DO THAT & THEN SOME

Transform Feelings of *Less Than* to *More Than Enough*

VICTORIA JOHNSON

This book is dedicated to every person who
has ever felt like they are not enough.

TABLE OF CONTENTS

FOREWORD

As a psychologist, I am passionate about understanding human emotions, unraveling personal stories, exploring untapped human potential, enhancing communication, strengthening personal and professional relationships and fostering emerging leadership. I understand how important it is to know that at the core we are all the same, and to have even our deepest thoughts and feelings validated.

In my practice, I have seen many people being stuck in limiting ways of thinking, feeling and being. The feeling of being *less than* can be debilitating. Often, they feel incapacitated to act and get trapped in cycles of anger, guilt, regret or shame. Many self-help books offer useful information but do not teach how to escalate out of limiting thoughts, feelings and behaviors. This book not only teaches readers to look within, but also gives point-by-point strategies on how to get to the point of feeling *more than enough*. This book goes beyond awareness and focuses on solutions and changes, that creates a wonderful movement forward. *Do That & Then Some: Transform Feelings Of Less Than To More Than Enough* puts the path of the reader's vision right into their own hands!

Victoria shares compelling stories based on her own personal life stories and those of her clients. Readers experience knowing that they are not alone in their thoughts or feelings of being *less than* and are shown the way to feeling *more than enough*. The book addresses beliefs formed in childhood, as well as better health and relationships, and more abundance and spiritual fulfillment.

As a colleague of Victoria, I am impressed with her strength as a leader as well as her genuine desire to guide people to self-healing. One of her strengths is how she holds the vision for her client until they are able to believe it for themselves.

Victoria's leadership, compassion, and sense of humor shine through in this book, as does her commitment to the reader. Her writing is entertaining, enlightening and empowering. She has exposed herself completely in this book by speaking her truth as a way to help others speak theirs. She has thoughtfully prepared a life guide that readers will refer to time and again.

If you've been looking for a modern and effective coaching book that can guide you through life's challenges to a permanent solution, this is it. This book is about getting you the results you want. If not now, when?

Sneha Shah
M.Sc. Psychology
M.S. Psychotherapy
Director ISRA Centre for Training – www.isra.co.in
Psychologist & Transformation Facilitator
Master of Business Administration
Diploma in Learning Disabilities

INTRODUCTION

Abandonment. Adoption. Small town preacher's kid. Teenage pregnancy. Failed marriages. Food banks. Cancer. You could say I've been through a lot.

Life lessons have made me a champion of overcoming pain and adversity. Instead of becoming a victim, I have turned my life experiences into love lessons that I share with my readers.

My life started out with abandonment and subsequent adoption. Recognizing that everyone can relate to being abandoned at some point in their life, I've dedicated my life to helping others to overcome and heal these feelings.

I've learned over the years that if these feelings of abandonment and rejection are left untreated and unresolved, they become the basis of how we make many of the choices in the blueprint of our life.

It is my passion to help others weave a beautiful and happy life by learning and growing from reading about my life experiences and in turn, for my readers to then use what they have learned as a catalyst to make changes in their own lives.

This is how *Do That & Then Some* was born. You will find it very relatable as it covers issues that are important to all of us, such as healing, health, relationships, prosperity, and spirituality.

I want you to know that you are no longer alone. You don't have to feel shame or anger about your own life experiences. *Do That & Then Some* will help you to heal, learn, grow and live the life you have always dreamed about and so rightly deserve.

SECTION ONE

YOUR INNER CHILD: YOUR DEFENDER OR YOUR DEMISE

CHAPTER 1

YOUR INNER CHILD
IS A SUPERHERO
(And deserves time off—with pay!)

I will admit to spending a solid week trying to come up with a better term than *inner child*. I thought it sounded too woowoo and that you, the reader, would tune it out or feel like you couldn't relate. I thought that my inner child was the only superhero out there who had been working full time for decades. After much thought, meditation and research, I remembered what I already knew—we are all the same.

Your inner child is there. Fancy scientific name or woowoo name, our inner child exists and is working full time trying to help us makes sense of every waking moment.

For those who are new to inner child work, let me take a moment to explain. Identifying the inner child was made mainstream many years ago by the influential works of Carl Jung and Emmet Fox who referred to the inner child as the Divine Child and the Wonder Child respectively. The inner child is a sub personality(ies) of our adult self. It is the part of our psyche that was developed in childhood and remains unchanged, molding us into the people that we are in our adult form. An example would be that if you were traumatized as a child through repeated behavior such as criticism, you will not react well to even the most constructive criticism from your friends, partner or boss until you have healed this area of the inner child.

This semi-independent child was formed in our youngest years when we were evolving and learning at superhuman rates. I will spare you from the science of it all, but study upon study proves that we do most of our learning in those early years under the age of seven. We learn behaviors that we play out over and over throughout our lives. That young learning can stay with us for a long time, as suggested in the example above.

If we had a childhood trauma that we could not cope with, it shows up in ways like sabotage and addiction in our adult lives. If you are not addicted to drugs, alcohol, food, sex or gambling, you may feel like you just dodged a bullet. Wait a minute—not so fast. Addiction shows up in sneaky ways, too, such as shopping, criticism, negative thinking, judging ourselves and others, food selection, exercise, codependency, and over-giving and over-working to name a few. Other ways this wounded child shows up is through bullying (yes, adults do it; but the inner child drives it). We wear masks or personas that seemingly protect the child but leave both our adult and child selves feeling like a fraud, lying habitually, and engaging in unhealthy sexual activity.

Your inner child is your defender and protector yet still wants your protection; they are the hero that makes you the champion, but they're also the catalyst for the destruction of relationships, goals, and satisfaction in life. Your inner child needs you to relinquish your secret shame and trauma, body image issues and negative self-talk so that they can get a day off. It's time.

Fear holds us back from making those changes. When we envision and affirm a new reality, we scare ourselves with all of the unknowns. As your defender and protector, your inner child suits up and is ready for battle even when it is against you—the one it is trying to protect.

One way my inner child shows up is by trying to pre-determine all of the variables and what-if's so that adult me feels more in control. I have been guilty of thinking of all the worst-case scenarios and letting fear set in and paralyze me in my day-to-day behaviors.

One night I lay in bed worrying because I knew my son was out for dinner and drinks. I thought about what would happen if he drank too much and made the decision to drive. *What if he got into an accident or was picked up by the police? What if he then lost his job, his wife, his family, his house* … and the list went on. I have learned to manage my emotions by being over-controlling, thanks to the skills learned by my inner child, who at this point would do anything for a good night's sleep—anything except for stopping her mission to protect me. Was my adult self genuinely willing to stay awake all night worrying about my son and what may or may not happen?

What if instead, I chose to banish my fear with light, action and faith? Addressing issues head on, taking them out of the shadows, shaking off the cobwebs, and shining a spotlight on them. In this scenario, it would mean letting go of my control and trusting that my son is an adult who makes healthy choices. As a side note, he was actually asleep at home, and I had imagined the whole scenario. I had let my fear drive my need for control. Two things remove the power of fear—exposing them to the light and showing love and compassion to the entire situation, including our inner child and grown-up selves. Do you know where fear cannot survive? In the light.

I can feel my inner child starting to protest—she keeps me physically and emotionally safe with her superpowers. She also bursts my dreams and holds me hostage thinking that she is protecting me. When I am willing to face my fears, I can stretch myself out of my comfort zone, knowing that my inner superhero is on my side because I have taken the time to listen to her concerns and address them accordingly.

When fear is brought to the light and doused with love, it allows us to explore self-knowledge and vulnerability. It allows us to be open, and talking about it takes away the shame and power. When our inner child and adult self

7

work together, we become the ultimate superhero in our own lives. We do this by showing courage and taking action. Sitting at home talking, complaining, and worrying is not action and only gives momentum to the villain—fear.

Join forces with your inner superhero and become an unstoppable force for good. Take the time to heal the inner child so that you are both prepared for your mission. Shine a light on your doubts, fears, worries, shoulds and what if's, so they are no match for the determination and strength you feel in your mission.

When my children were young, we used to watch a cartoon called *Inspector Gadget*. It featured an accident-prone detective, the brain behind solving the crimes—his dog, and niece Penny. Each episode, Inspector Gadget would be assigned a mission and would set out to solve the case. He would get side-tracked, follow the wrong clues, and find the longest and most difficult path to the solution. If it were not for his dog and Penny, he would still be wandering around strategizing his next move on his first assignment. When he aligned with Penny, most of the problem solving was done without him noticing, he accomplished his mission, and Penny was gracious enough to let him take the credit. Think of your relationship with your inner child like that of Inspector Gadget and Penny. And just in case there was ever any doubt; you are the detective in this example, not Penny or the dog.

Don't talk yourself into waiting until you are ready. Start before you have everything perfect. You can change things to just how you like them as you go along. You will adapt as you grow and evolve, so waiting until you have everything as you want it is pointless. The most important thing is to create momentum in the direction of your mission.

Be an excuse buster, and listen to your thoughts and words. The best teacher you will ever have is you. You are the one with personal experience. You are the one who will learn from your mistakes. You are the one who knows what resonates with you and will tweak your plans over and over on the way to completing your mission. Do that.

And then some:

1. Get very clear on what your mission is and write it down. When you are specific, it creates emotions. For example, "I am going to order pasta" compared to "I am going to order lasagna and have them bake it in the oven so that the cheese on top is extra crispy."

2. Be ready. Do the inner work necessary to make sure that little superhero is on the same track as you and will be assisting in the mission. Do the same for the adult superhero. If you don't know how to do this, keep reading and hire a personal coach. Contact me for recommendations.

3. Be so committed to your plan that no backup plan is necessary.

4. Be ready to laugh at yourself when you act like Inspector Gadget.

5. To keep yourself accountable, write down your action plan.

6. Then write down what it will be like when you achieve your mission. Be very specific. Write down what your ideal day would be like, as well as your average day.

7. Stay completely focused on manifesting your mission and believing it to be true. When your superhero is on board, you are destined for success.

CHAPTER 2

WHEN YOUR PAST IS STILL PULLING THE TRIGGER

(This will go a lot better for you if you lower your weapon and cooperate.)

The fastest way for me to be triggered is when I see someone doing something that I don't like about myself. Even when I think I have worked through the emotion, it comes back with lightning speed and force when the action is reflected back to me. When I see traits in the other person that I don't like about myself, my first reflex is to point and blame. And not at myself. As long as I can point out what others are doing wrong, I don't have to look at me. Can you relate to this?

When we see a person acting in a way we think is weak and we don't like it, it is often because we don't like when we show weakness. Powerful people want other people to be powerful and can't comprehend why they would show weakness. The truth is, weakness is the powerful person's biggest fear. It is terrifying to see other people showing vulnerability. Rather than explore that emotion, the powerful person brands the other as weak or as acting like a victim. This causes separation and provides us with weapons to use against each other.

This seems to be a common factor in our society when our past is still controlling our present. We seek external validation, and we do not honor ourselves. We gossip, tell little white lies, and compete. We are programmed to believe if you get yours, there won't be enough for me. This is not healthy competition but rather—*I am gonna take you down for mirroring that thing I am most afraid of.*

When people seek external validation and don't receive it, they often turn to addiction. It doesn't have to be drugs, alcohol, or cigarettes. As noted in Chapter 1, addiction wears clever disguises. It can be working, exercising, obsessive eating, obsessiveness about what we eat, or simply being addicted to being busy 24/7.

We take on too much. We feel invisible. We look for relief.

Addictions influence not only the individual with the addiction, but also their family. Over time, destructive patterns are created, and the people involved become victims to the role they have gradually learned to play out.

Addictions are developed over time. What starts out as something for enjoyment, or relief from stress, evolves into an overwhelming need, creating the addict. An addict rarely admits to the severity of the addiction; however they still experience shame, guilt and disappointment in themselves. They live with low self-esteem and repeatedly sabotage their own efforts to break free from what is controlling them.

Even though they are well-meaning, they become unreliable. The addict develops behavioral problems as the voice of the addiction (their thoughts) becomes louder than their good intentions. When an addict is overcome by their desires, they lose sight of what is important to them.

Often, we pick up these addictions when trying to carry all of the responsibility for our families, shielding them from reality. Eventually the addiction causes conflict within the family. As a result, family members learn to behave in a reactional pattern, and a new family dynamic is formed. Yes. This is natural but—in the end—counter-productive.

Yvonne is a coaching client who I have counseled for her addiction for the last few years. She is a single mother and the youngest daughter in a large family. Each person in Yvonne's family fulfills a role. The chief enabler is Yvonne's mother; the hero, her older sister. The scapegoat is Yvonne's middle sister. The lost child is Yvonne's youngest daughter, and Yvonne's oldest daughter is the mascot.

The hero has been negotiating with the addict for several years. She sees what is happening and feels responsible for fixing the pain of the addict and the family. The hero is high functioning and portrays the image of a healthy and stable family unit. Inside, however, the hero is often scared and hurting. She feels alone in her quest to save the family. Occasionally, Yvonne will cooperate with the hero by admitting herself to seek counseling. More often than not, Yvonne is then 'saved' by the chief enabler who will assure her that she has everything under control and that they don't need outside help, which reinforces Yvonne's denial. The chief enabler is the most damaging person in this scenario.

The enabler inserts herself into the addict's life, caring for her and her children, as a way to feed her own need for normalcy and self-worth. This validates Yvonne's actions and enables her to continue them. The mascot keeps her mother and grandmother distracted and amused with a false sense of happiness. This further masks the pain within the family. The chief enabler and the mascot become Yvonne's closest confidantes, both willing to conceal the problems within the family.

The mascot's needs are unmet and unacknowledged by the other family members, because she sends out the message that everything is fine—that she's alright. The lost child is unseen in this family. She stays under the radar of the other members as her way of coping and diminishing the family's pain. She is depressed and lonely and has developed low self-esteem as a result of the lack of attention.

The lost child and the scapegoat have deep feelings of emotional abandonment. The scapegoat is determined and appears strong. She has been neglected by the enabler and has existed in Yvonne's shadow for years. As a sister and a daughter, she feels like nothing she ever does is good enough—or bad enough—and seeks out ways to get noticed. The scapegoat is vulnerable to addiction herself and commits herself fully to whatever behavior she takes on. Ironically, the scapegoat is often the one who breaks the cycle of dysfunction because she has developed the most skills and confidence. She learned early on that she needed to depend on herself to survive.

These patterns developed gradually but are now repeated daily. They lead to generational dysfunction due to the underlying emotions of each person and role described in the scenario. These individuals are rarely aware of what is really going on, hence they tend to keep doing more of the same or intensifying the actions they are already taking in a more and more desperate attempt to solve the problem.

The entire family is more susceptible to abuse, both physical and emotional, than families that live outside of the sharp curves, rises and falls of addiction. The cycles and patterns make them victims of not only Yvonne's behavior, but of their own. They think negatively toward themselves and others. Subsequently, those thoughts then become their behaviors, and ultimately their experiences.

In this example alone, there is the potential for each role to attract and be comfortable raising a family that emulates this model. The patterns of codependency are deeply grooved into their lifestyle choices.

Skilled family counselors will be able to identify the roles played by their clients like Yvonne and her family. The counselor can then assist in altering the way their client reacts to day-to-day situations.

If you can relate to the above example of addiction, perhaps you can identify your role within the family when you are under stress. The inner child in most of us was told to be good. We were taught to want everyone to like us. Recognize that what both the child and the adult really want is to drop their defenses and stop relying on addiction, fight-or-flight responses and stress to get them through the day. Lower your weapon. Do that.

And then some:

1. We are afraid of imperfection and we hold ourselves to a standard much higher than we would hold anyone else. It is a serious epidemic in our society. Practice saying no to others in order to say yes to yourself.

2. Do less. You want to be able to give to people but pull back first in order to do a personal inventory of your needs and desires.

3. Carve out some space in your life to find out who

you really are. Journal and list what is important to you so that you can learn to know yourself and your desires.

4. Give up on perfection. Failure is your friend; it teaches you lessons. Lessons do not need to keep repeating or fuel an addictive personality. They can simply teach what you need to know in the moment if you are able to let go of your emotional attachment to them.

5. Let go of your expectations of others and you will experience less disappointment. Remember that we are all the same. There is a line in *The Color Purple* that states: "Everything that is done to you has already been done to me." We are all scared of being invisible and we are all scared of really being seen for who we are. When we let go of our unrealistic expectations and demands on ourselves, we can let go of them for others as well. This is key to your inner peace and healing.

CHAPTER 3

I DESERVE TO BE LEFT

(I mean loved. I deserve to be loved! And so do you.)

I remember being at a workshop and the writing instructor asking the participants to think of something about which we could never write. I will share with you one of the two topics that I identified. The tears are welling up in my eyes at the very thought of putting all of these feelings into words. It somehow makes them even more real, and frankly, at this moment, I would like to keep them safely under lock and key. I fear that unlocking this box will be painful, but an even larger fear is the fear of not sharing this experience that I truly believe will help others. It is about shame and rejection, something we have all felt in some form.

I once heard a lecture from Dr. Bruce Lipton, a renowned stem cell biologist, geneticist and former professor, in which he explained that the emotions of the mother alter the fetus's DNA, brain development, and well-being. As a side note, if you haven't read *The Biology of Belief* by Dr. Bruce Lipton, be sure to put it on your list!

He made a believer out of me.

I digress. I feel the avoidance of getting to where I am going because I don't want to address the subject of shame. Shame is not a pretty topic, nor is rejection or loss. But here we go.

I have had shame issues my entire life. When I heard Dr. Lipton speak, it resonated with me because I am confident that my birth mother experienced shame throughout her pregnancy. If I have the story correct (as told to me by my birth father who has since passed away), I was conceived on the night that my birth father's wife died. He had been with my mother, and he was driving back to the hospital when he felt an overwhelming sense of loss and then arrived at the hospital to hear the news of his wife's passing. My birth mother was the very young girl next door who helped out with babysitting the couple's three daughters. I recognize that this story paints my birth father in a poor light. I have no excuses for him nor do I claim to understand how this happened. I only know that I feel protective of him, even though the series of events paints a different picture.

My birth parents both felt extreme shame about my birth mother's pregnancy. She internalized that shame and felt it externally as well, as her family and community held judgment against her. She was a teenager raised in an alcoholic home and felt that she was without a support system. After my birth, she brought me into the home of my birth father and his deceased wife and their three daughters and tried to make us all a family. My birth mother claims that I was the perfect child who never cried and was so sweet and lovable. Yet, six months later, I was surrendered to Children's Aid to be placed up for adoption. My birth father claims to have not known about this and just came home to a house in which both she and I were missing.

I spent a few months in an orphanage and was then adopted by a loving family who wished to bring me home and provide a younger sister for their daughter. It sounds like a happy ending, but it was only the beginning of the unshakable sorrow that I have carried my entire life. It may not seem logical, but I assure you it is real and has been a driving force behind years of self-rejection, self-loathing and low self-esteem.

Fast forward eighteen years to when I held my own child in my arms as a single mother. As this sweet boy reached the same age that I was when I was given away, I recognized the rage inside me for the first time. Up until then, I always believed she must have had a good reason to give me away. How could anyone walk away from a child such as this, I asked myself over and over. I internalized that I must have been too much to handle, too hard to love, and not important enough to keep.

I knew that I would have done anything to keep my child safe, and at no point did I ever consider that protecting a child would possibly mean separating that child from its mother. Separation was inconceivable at any age, but especially at this age.

I knew my son knew who his family was; he missed me when I was away for an hour or two, seeing me comforted him, and my sweet little boy trusted me. How could leaving that child with an agency ever be considered the best possible option? Again, my self-worth plummeted to nothing.

Every situation has its unique circumstances. I don't pretend to know what life would have been like if my mother hadn't walked away from me that day. What I do know is what life was like because she did. At fifty-two years old, and with over thirty years of counseling and self-help strategies behind me, I am still feeling the shame of it.

I was twenty-three when I was reunited with my birth family. My birth parents had gotten married and had three more children. My birth mother and I traveled to the city of my birth. We visited the house we lived in as a family. We stood in the back alley overlooking the backyard of my parents' home, with her parents' home right next door.

She showed me the handprints of my sisters, preserved in the cement sidewalk when it was still wet and moldable, and then said, "I was standing right here when they took you from me." She told a story about how an older neighbor lady was helping her and had suggested she would be better off getting away from my dad, and I would be better off being given up for adoption. I felt a surge of rage, but being a nice girl, I suppressed it.

My birth mother then expressed guilt and sorrow for having relinquished me but never admitted her responsibility in the decision. My rage bubbled again. During the previous months, I had been so absorbed in comforting her in her grief and regret that I forgot about that sweet baby girl who was passed from her arms into the arms of a stranger.

I remember being aware of the pile of chopped wood that I was standing beside and how I wanted to throw each piece of wood and smash everything in sight. Instead, I cried briefly, composed myself, and carried on, reassuring her and claiming that I was fine.

Fast forward another few decades, and we are both still hiding behind 'fine.' I keep my rage active without even knowing that I am doing it because it remains carefully under lock and key. My birth mother has come in and out of my life several times now. Over the last few years, she has been everything you would expect from a distant relative. She sends cards faithfully for all of the annual occasions. She expresses a desire to see me and tells me how much she misses me. These words are nice to hear, but they are hollow. I don't trust them. I am working on it.

I want so badly to believe her words. Even after all of these years, I still have the young child in me who is wanting the unconditional love and acceptance of her mother. I am scared to commit without having an 'out' in my mind; my process is that it is far better to reject first, rather than to feel the pain of rejection again. The truth is that by holding on to my story of rejection I keep hurting myself, and she is not responsible for that. I am doing that to myself.

Many of my relationships imploded because I chose people who were not capable of loving me unconditionally. Added to the poor choices, I held a core belief that I am hard to love, and people walking away from me became my status quo. I expected it, and it happened.

When it comes to my relationship with my birth mother, I have given all I can give and still feel like it is not enough. Loving her and wanting her love has been my strongest weakness. Even though I am older and more experienced in this dynamic, my inner child still wants a mother to love and to feel loved by her mother.

I now recognize—usually—when both of our behaviors are questionable at best and narcissistic at worst. I have set boundaries to protect myself and do my best not to hurt myself when internalizing the story of my need for protection. The walls are made of the thinnest paper and could easily collapse inward, so I diligently practice ways of improving my self-worth and affirming that I am lovable and worth loving on a daily basis. I remind myself that I need not be ashamed of who I am.

I remember that I am valuable and that—with practice—forgiveness, understanding and love will become my default reaction. I also remember that it is better to be angry than to be 'fine' and that it is healthy to express that anger appropriately when it shows up in the day to day of my life experience. Do that.

And then some:

1. Do you have a pattern of rejection that keeps repeating itself in your life? Write down the commonalities of each situation.

2. Determine your deservability level. Have you always put yourself second (or last)? What do you feel you deserve in your personal relationships?

3. Do you give to receive? Are you loving and kind to those around you in hopes of convincing them to be loving and kind to you in return? Do you accept their misbehavior because you want their love? This behavior points to a self-worth problem that can be overcome by practicing daily meditation and affirmations.

4. Dig deep into the very root of the issue. Did this start in childhood? Is there someone you can discuss it with who would provide a safe place for you?

5. Does that someone deserve your confidence and trust? If not, write a letter, or have a conversation with yourself out loud.

6. Dig deeper. Find the root and expose it. Once you

can see it in the light of day, you can respond from a place of knowledge.

7. Protect and heal the child within you. I don't care how grown up and important you are, that little one is still in there. And all that inner child wants and needs is love and acceptance to heal.

CHAPTER 4

LET IT GO. SERIOUSLY, IT'S TIME.
(Or at least stop talking about it.)

It is a choice to see yourself as broken. Whether you have been doing it since childhood or if it is new to you, you are not broken. And if you are cracked, you are fixable. You can choose a different version of how you see yourself and the world you live in. We learned at a young age not to touch a hot stove. If we did it once, that was the only lesson we needed. As adults, we let our inner child push our emotional hot buttons by touching the flame over and over, never quite allowing the pain to heal before new blisters are formed.

Some people can tell the story of the troubled times in their life with the finesse of a master storyteller. They are committed so deeply that they can fill in all the details with ease and grace, using the perfect inflection to get the greatest response from the listener.

For example, one such storyteller might say:

"Ten years ago my marriage broke up. My partner lied to me and cheated on me. My children and I were destroyed, and our family just exploded in a moment. It was totally out of our control and unexpected. There was nothing left but pain and betrayal. I am so angry that this happened to me. I had to raise the children alone and sometimes things were tough. I had no child support and very little emotional support. People tell me that I should forgive my ex and move on, but why would I forgive them after what happened? My ex hasn't even apologized. Now the best years of my life are over and I am too tired to pursue another relationship. I'm going to grow old alone. I guess that's the way it is going to be in my life even though I didn't do anything wrong."

The storyteller is rewarded by getting to be the victim each time this version of the story is retold. (And believe me when I say, this type of person tells it often.) It has become a big part of the definition of who that person is as a whole. If you continue speaking to them, you will find that they have an entire repertoire of such stories. They identify themselves as separate from other people. They typecast themselves in the role of a victim who is not worthy of love.

An alternative version of the same story could be:

"My marriage broke up for a number of reasons, including betrayal. We were not communicating and were not on the same page in our sense of love and family. It was very painful at the time, but I have worked through it. I have been blessed in many ways because of our marriage ending. My children and I have always been very close, and I was free to move forward and create a better life for us all. When the time is right, I know I will meet the right person for me."

Compare the energy of each version of the same story. The first one is filled with stress, negativity, and victimization. The second tells of life experiences and not only shows the storyteller's growth but allows the reader to learn and grow themselves. This version is filled with wisdom and hope for the future. It makes you feel lighter while reading it and attracts the reader to the storyteller instead of having you look for the nearest exit as in the first story.

When you recognize that you are the creator of your life story, you can catch yourself when you are getting drawn back into the version in which you are the victim. There are certain events which you can't change, but you can always change your perception of the events. You can choose a happier memory just like you can select a healthier thought.

Each time you are in a difficult situation or are recalling an event from your past, you have the choice of perception. You can be a victim of your own story or a student of it, merely by altering your thoughts.

If your inner child is still reliving the trauma of the event, this is not always easy to do. That inner voice wants to stomp its feet and convince you that something has been done to you. The inner child remembers the separation that it felt in its developmental stages and how the abandoning by your spouse felt the same way.

The wounded inner child wants you to feel separate from your true self and from other people rather than feeling a sense of belonging only to have it taken away. The US Army Medical Department has observed that symptoms of post-traumatic stress disorder (PTSD) are retriggered in the telling of the traumatic event. Imagine reliving your trauma over and over by choice, keeping yourself stuck in the pattern of both physical and emotional stress.

Can you understand why your inner child has resorted to tantrums to change your perception? A child of trauma only knows trauma, and the normalization of the day-to-day routine feels unsafe. The inner child knows that it is just a matter of time until the next event and desires to protect you from it. Think of it as the child who is saying "How dare you move on with your life and leave me here with all of this pain and suffering?" Your response can be simple. "I am choosing to create new memories for us both. I will keep you safe. You can trust me. I am releasing us both from the past so that we can create a future that is good for us both." Do that.

And then some:

1. Instead of being stuck in the past, you can choose to refer to your higher self and your inner wisdom so you can rise above any life event.

2. The hurt will stay with you until you accept and release this situation. You can choose to heal from it by practicing willingness to release the blame and anger and replace them with higher emotions such as forgiveness and acceptance.

3. Do this by writing a letter to all parties involved, and then meditate until you can feel a sense of letting go and relief. Proclaim out loud, "I release you and set myself free." Destroy the letter.

4. Let go of what you can't control by choosing to focus on what you can. Check your thoughts often throughout the day to check on your focus.

5. Forgiveness, letting go, and acceptance are like muscles that need to be exercised. Start with something small to build those muscles, and work your way up to forgiving the more traumatic events.

6. Practice finding the positive in all situations. Everything worth having takes practice. Eventually, a positive response will be your default response. In the keeping of the metaphor, your training will translate into not having a build-up of lactic acid and subsequently there will no more sore muscles. You will be on your way to being emotionally fit, stretching your mind to think in a new pattern, and enjoying the benefits of your labor.

CHAPTER 5

THE THINGS OF WHICH
WE DO NOT SPEAK

(Own them or they own you.)

I recently spent the Saturday before Father's Day planting flowers on the graves of my adoptive parents. Both of them were amazing people who showed their love to me in very different ways. Dad was soft and kind; Mom was strict, but she modeled truth and integrity and was respected as a leader in our community.

I had my partner and my granddaughter who is seven with me. After planting the flowers, we went to my grandparents' graves, sat down, and unpacked a picnic lunch. My granddaughter is so at home in the cemetery and has always been comfortable with the idea of death. She was her usual animated and bubbly self. I opened my sparkling water, and it sprayed all over my shirt, causing her to laugh so hard that she fell over. This child can feel joy anywhere. She is safe and protected and knows that she has a family who adores her. She is encouraged to express her feelings, and if that is hysterical laughter in a cemetery—well then, that is the perfect place.

My eighty-year-old aunt came walking up carrying an old margarine container that had held water for flowers at her husband's grave on the far side of the cemetery. She also had some metal flowers for her father's grave. It seems that even when you are eighty, and your father has been gone for three decades, you can still feel the loss.

My father has been gone for a year as I write this. I miss him like crazy every day. There is a hole in my life that no other man will ever be able to fill. He was thoughtful and gentle. He always treated me with kindness. I spent my life loving this man who snuck me food when I was sent to my room without dinner and didn't care if I got dirty. He had a simple life, and he had his priorities right. He didn't have a lot of tolerance for people who were different than him—until he understood, and then he never forgot to appreciate what made them different. Don't get me wrong, he prequalified others as many people of his generation do, but he enjoyed them. (For example, they are Catholics, but they are really lovely people!)

I tried to discuss the hurts from my childhood and teenage years with him on a few occasions. This gentle man would respond with volatile anger if I expressed memories he didn't want to hear. I learned to do what I felt safe doing. I wrote.

I wrote about my shame, and I read him my deepest secrets. I let him have time. He gave me what felt like silent anger. His heart-wrenching regret and apology followed. He was sorry for not knowing what my life was like for all of those years. We never spoke of it again.

Maybe that is all the discussion that was needed. The feeling different. The separation. The trauma, the wrong decisions, the results. Perhaps the only light they required was that moment. Maybe that was the best way for us both to cope. Maybe it wasn't.

As a child of adoption, I already felt different. Separate. Then I had a caregiver feeding me ideas that I was not wanted, and that my adoptive mother wasn't much of a mother, further fueling the feelings of isolation. I established early on that I was not good enough and would have to work harder than other people to have the minimum amount of love and acceptance in my life.

I found safety in food. The one thing that was always there for me. Food was the thing I could count on no matter what I was feeling. More accurately, the one thing that could disconnect me from what I was feeling. I established the pattern of eating my feelings early on in childhood. I also believed that I was not a priority to anyone, so I was not a priority to myself either. This belief carried on throughout most of my life until I learned to love myself.

As a child, I learned that being sneaky was a must, and that love always had conditions. As a teenager, this skewed thinking was disastrous. I often found myself in dangerous situations, and believe me, the last thing I would have ever done was ask for help. I thought I was an outsider and on my own. That may not have been the reality, but it was my belief, so it was my reality. I lived my teens, twenties and thirties in this illusion. A pattern was established, and I repeated it for decades.

I have to be accountable for that. No one else.

Yup. You read that. Me, myself and I. That is who is responsible for the choices I made as an adult. Yes, things could have been smoother for me as a child. Yes, that could have set me on a different course for my life. No, that doesn't let me off the hook.

I got pregnant as a teenager with someone who didn't care at all about me. Looking back, I didn't care about me either. That was my responsibility. I did that. Then, at nineteen, I married the next guy who talked to me (almost literally). He turned out to be a poor choice, too. My responsibility. I was stuck in what I thought I 'should' do. I should stay married; I should make this work, my son should have a father, being married is forever, God doesn't accept divorce and remarriage, and so on. I did everything I could to be more lovable. I worked more; I hung out with my husbands friends more. I accepted drinking and hanging out with older people in their garage like it was something 'winners' do. When I came home to find my husband in bed with someone, well that was his responsibility, but my reaction was all on me.

34

I could have made meaningful choices on how to be influenced, rather than be controlled by my emotions and therefore wholly reactive. Instead of reacting with violence and a bottle of pills in the bottom of my stomach, I could have made choices to end the chaotic marriage when I saw the signs—the flashing neon, eye-catching signs. Instead, I put on blinders and went back to medicating with food.

After many weeks of psychiatric evaluation, group counseling, and tolerating people praying for me, I felt like I could get my life back on track. I say 'tolerated' because I felt like it was a superiority move—like their life was on track so they could pray for mine. It didn't feel like my life anymore, but it felt like what society expected it to be, so I played along as long as I could.

Over time, I heard all the silent 'shoulds' that were only in my head, in full voice from my mother. The reasons why my marriage failed. Dinner was not on the table every night; the house was not clean enough, and so on.

I wanted to scream my truth. My excuses, my reasons. The trauma from my childhood and teen years—the things that my parents exposed me to and left me open to because they didn't know about the evil in the world—those things were in my marriage, too. They were part of the demise. I will still own that. The choices I made. I will own that. And I will always remember a discussion with my adoptive mother standing in my doorway. It was the one time she acknowledged the truth of what I had endured. But from that day on, it remained the thing of which we do not speak. In a way, it still owns me, and I am working on that.

Looking back, I can see that the little child in me who needed security also needed a voice. The teenager who was looking for love, and finding everything except love, needed a voice. A strong, steady friend to guide her. Over time, and now every time, I have learned to be that friend. Do that.

And then some:

1. Go back in your mind to identify childhood trauma. If possible, find a picture of that child and cherish it close. Love that child.

2. In a safe space, imagine yourself loving that child, providing his/her need to be loved, safe and supported. Love that child.

3. Identify belief patterns that the child has and when, why and how they became established. Ask questions, find out what is really true. Love that child.

4. In your mind, love and support that child through their teenage years and into adulthood. Let him/her know that you will always be there for them.

5. Take responsibility for the choices you have made in your life, no matter what. If you are reading this, you

are too old to be blaming anyone, including yourself. Just take responsibility, recognize the patterns in your life, and choose to move on. It is a choice; the past only exists in your mind.

6. Be kind to yourself. Accept that as you know better in life, you do better. Check in with that child, teenager, and young adult daily. Let them know that you accept them and that they are whole.

7. Know that all parts of you are lovable and let go of guilt and shame and replace them with daily doses of love and approval. You do not have to earn love; you were born worthy.

CHAPTER 6

THEY SAY DEPRESSION IS "A DIP."
(Um, no. It's more like Drowning.)

My inner child has a lot of experience with depression. I am not even sure at what age she started repressing her feelings, pretending to be someone she wasn't, and putting on a brave face to try and be like other people. I have a picture of myself that was taken around the age of four. I remember the day; I remember that I knew that being myself was not good enough, and that if I wanted to be loved, I needed to morph into what others wanted from me. Expressing my feelings was not an option. In most families that I was exposed to, the phrase 'Children are to be seen and not heard' was not implied but verbalized. When fear, loneliness and anger are not expressed, they show up in other ways. For me it was with over-eating and depression.

In my mid-thirties, I seemed to have conquered the depression cycles and went many years without it showing up again. But as we have been learning in this section, when that inner child has unresolved issues, you can bet on them showing up over and over in our lifetimes.

I have been aware of depression trying to sneak back in as I have been writing this book. As I type these words, I wonder if I will be brave enough to follow through. The answer comes to me quickly; this book is about helping others. I have to be real and honest to do that, so here I am. I am showing up, looking for the same things you are, to understand myself more, and to grow.

I was medicated for depression from my teenage years to my mid-thirties. When I found the medication was only suppressing and dulling all of my feelings—the highs and the lows—I turned to counseling. Counseling was very effective for many years, but then a few years ago, I experienced a major trauma that brought back all of those childhood feelings, plus a dump truck full of guilt. I began to see a therapist who specialized in inner child work. (What was I thinking?) Facing down many of my fears, I cried, kicked, screamed and even vomited in her garbage can, and thought that once and for all I was learning to really feel my feelings.

As depression increases, so does my shame, embarrassment and feelings of failure. Throughout this latest episode, I have remained unmedicated and let the inner child have free reign over my self-talk. I have since recognized the depression was triggered by criticism and comparison, lack of recognition, and favoritism—all things that inner child of mine is highly sensitive to. (God bless her.)

The reel in my head runs like this: Victoria, you are a successful coach and teacher. You teach other people to love themselves more every single day. You do affirmations, you teach affirmations, you do visualizations, you teach visualizations, you practice meditation, you encourage others to practice meditation. You know and you teach that if you change your thoughts, you change your life. If you have depression, that means that you are a 100 % hypocrite and failure.

Then, I switch to the second track: Victoria, you have every reason to be happy. You have several successful businesses, a man who adores you and treats you like gold, a family who loves you, six amazing grandchildren, all of the freedom anyone could ever want, and still, you are depressed. What is wrong with you? Why can't you be happy with what you have?

Track 3: Everyone is watching you and judging you. It is easy to see when you are failing because you gain weight and the whole world can see. You can fake it and smile all you want, but everyone knows. Pull your act together. At least make it look like all is well on the outside. Jeez. Get it together, girl.

Track 4: I can't do it. I'm scared. I don't know why I can't lose the weight, shake off the feelings of being overwhelmed, let go of stress, be a nicer partner, save more money, and all of the other things I judge myself for being and thinking. Why can't I be happy like everyone else?

Then in the midst of the darkness comes a new track.

Track 5: It's okay, honey. It's okay to have depression; you don't have to be ashamed. It's okay to be overwhelmed; you are amazing to me. It's okay to be exactly who you are. Who you are is who you are meant to be. What you think of as flaws are just part of what makes you the person that you are. You have always been so competitive; maybe it is time to cut yourself a break and stop comparing yourself to others. Remember that you teach people to help them accept themselves right where they are at the present moment. If I could ask one thing of you, it would be to find some compassion for yourself. You don't need to hold yourself to a higher standard than you would hold others. You are a teacher because you are a student and riding these waves in life. Sometimes that wave will bring depression, and sometimes it will bring joy, and it is all okay. It's okay to be who you are today. Just be you. It's okay; everything you feel is okay.

Amidst all the tears of the new track, I feel nurtured. I feel as if that ashamed adult has connected with the precious little girl inside who wants to feel her feelings. She is tired of fighting and wants to be the best she can be—naturally and without a struggle so that she can shine.

I recognize now that sometimes the best that I can be is overweight, depressed and stressed. That's alright because each moment gives me an opportunity to accept a kinder, more loving thought. When the time is right, my spirits will be lifted by my thoughts, and the thoughts will turn into actions. I am willing to accept that and to trust in the timing of the Universe. On days that I can't quite do that, I am willing to be willing. Undoubtedly, I am willing to accept that I am not alone. Do that.

And then some:

1. Remember that the Universe, God, your Higher Power, always has a plan for you and wants what is best for you. Even when you want to give up, your Source will not give up on you.

2. Accept what you are feeling. That doesn't permit you to stay there forever. If you accept what you are feeling, you are free to reach for the higher thought, get professional help, and speak to your friends, family or support tribe about your feelings. There are free resources for this at www.victoriajohnson.org that will help you accept your feeling and reach for the higher thought.

3. Let go of the shame.

4. Practice self-compassion. Picture yourself as a young girl or boy who needs nurturing, love and acceptance. Use your adult self to connect with that younger self and let them know that they are safe, accepted, and heard.

5. Whether you are depressed, stressed, anxious or_____ (and the list goes on and on), learn to accept where you are without self-judgment.

6. Know that you are enough. Let go of the story that you are only enough when you are at your best. You are also enough when you are facing challenges. You are enough. Period. End of story. You are enough; you are worth loving.

7. No matter what. You are worthy; you are enough. Yes, you. Embrace the affirmation, *I am enough exactly as I am.*

SECTION TWO

YOUR HEALTH: USING YOUR
THOUGHTS, FEELINGS, AND
EMOTIONS TO IMPROVE IT

CHAPTER 7

THE SCALE DOES NOT MEASURE YOUR VALUE

(You are Pure Gold, and That $hit is Heavy!)

One morning I woke up in a hotel room and wandered into the bathroom to get ready for the day. The bathroom had bright overhead pot lights illuminating a wall-size mirror. I looked up and was startled. I was barely recognizable to myself. I looked puffy and as if I had somehow been inflated overnight. I tried making different faces to recognize myself but was unable to find the person I see in my mind's eye when I visualize myself. I had been through some health challenges over the previous months which had made it difficult to exercise or eat real food. It was a vicious cycle of feeling poorly but not having the energy to take control. Instead, I spiraled downward emotionally, and my weight shot up concurrently. Over the past few weeks, I had been feeling much better physically, and now my state of mind was waking up to my new physical reality. It was startling.

Later that morning I arrived at the motivational conference where I was volunteering. As a certified coach and facilitator, this was the third consecutive year that I'd been chosen to represent the Heal Your Life information booth based on Louise Hay's bestselling book, *You Can Heal Your Life*. The irony was forefront in my mind as I smiled and encouraged others.

Someone wanted a picture with me and then posted it to Facebook. I saw the full-length picture on the Heal Your Life Facebook page and felt shame. Although I felt confident and passionate about the work that I was promoting, I was battling a familiar and judgmental inner voice. My inner critic. The voice that tells me I am not good enough and that I am a fraud, because I wasn't able to heal my own life with a 50+ pound weight gain that is out there for everyone to see. This is not the first time I have been down this road. The old shame and self-loathing were back like old friends to make sure that my misery had company.

Throughout the day I was able to wander in and out of lectures by world-renowned speakers, authors and teachers. While everyone was in conference, there was no activity at my booth, so I could slip in the back and hear little pieces of wisdom. Barbara De Angelis spoke on soul accomplishments and used the example of: "Today I choose to forgive myself for something I have been beating myself up for." I realized at that moment that I had been doing exactly what I coach other people not to do. Self-criticism doesn't work. If it did, we would all be skinny and wealthy with no unhealthy habits and with perfect relationships. I also realized I had been evaluating myself by what can be measured on the outside and not the inside.

Colette Baron-Reid spoke of our transformations and encouraged us to be patient with ourselves. She spoke of the judgmental voices that we hear in our minds and referred to them as the strange hitchhikers in the back seat of our car. We all have stories; they don't have to define us.

It seemed that I was being Divinely guided to hear precisely what I needed to hear to focus on for my personal healing. To wrap up the day I was able to catch a few words from Dr. Robert Holden. Again, I felt like he said them just for me. He was part of the Dove Campaign for Real Beauty and asked the question: "When did you stop thinking you were beautiful?" For many of us, the answer will be in our youngest school days. He spoke of spiritual intelligence and finding out the heart of who we *really* are, not who we *think* we are or what we *think* others expect us to be. His message was that we think that we are our bodies—not that we have bodies. His example was: "I am fat." We can insert whatever resonates with us after the words "I am _____." How can we see our eternal loveliness and grace if we fill in the blank with a judgment about our bodies? There are better ways to express who we are as a whole being.

Fast forward a couple of years. I had let go of some of the metaphorical weight I had been carrying and decided it was time to go hardcore on reducing my physical weight. I started an eating plan that I did not deviate from for even a moment. Not one morsel from the *do not eat* list had passed my lips for seven weeks. I felt genuine fear standing naked in front of the scale in my bedroom. I was about to measure my self-worth.

There was no change on the scale.

I got dressed and went into the other room where my partner waited for the big news. No change. He was shocked and ran out to the store to buy another scale. (God bless this man.) He came home, and I went back into the bedroom with both scales, stripped down, carefully removing my glasses and my socks to be sure I would get the maximum weight loss measurement.

I stared at both scales, the evil one and the one that gave me hope. No change. Time stood still. "How can this be?" I asked myself under my breath. I felt healthier, more in tune with my body, dare I say even beautiful. How could the scale—my lifelong measuring device—argue with that?

My mood plummeted, and the crazy talk started up quickly and eloquently. My healthy confidence was replaced by frustration and anger. It was as though I thought I could lower the number on the scale by using criticism and self-loathing talk. Whoa, I recognized this

49

road. I had filled the potholes in before; I did not need to re-pave it now. I needed to take a new road.

Getting dressed, I left the bedroom and took the first scale with me. I walked straight through the house and out the front door to the garbage can, leaving my partner to do what he pleased with the second 'self-worth' scale that he had so kindly just purchased for me. I continued walking and went to work in my backyard, trimming the trees that my dad had planted and groomed with love.

It was there that I remembered that—like the trees—my body responds to the seasons in my life. There are seasons that I am healthier and more productive; there are seasons that are not. Does the tree ever stop being a tree because it has no fruit? No, it just accepts what is, and knows that soon there will be new leaves, blossoms and fruits.

I started to think about what a spectacular being my body is. Like the fruit tree, it has many parts that make it whole. What if I stopped questioning my physical self and instead practiced immeasurable gratitude for each of the organs that support me by doing their thing 24/7/365? What if instead of looking for cellulite, I began to show appreciation for the legs that carry me, and for the arms and hands that do exactly what I want them to do. The same for the eyes that see, ears that hear, nose, taste buds and all of the spectacular wonders of my body. When I look at the whole me, it is inconceivable to think I could measure my worth on a weigh scale.

Now, I choose to look in the mirror and admire who is reflected back at me. All of me. I see my outer beauty, and the inner grace physically, mentally, emotionally and spiritually. Sure, if I had a magic wand with an eraser I could remove a few lines and bumps, but I would never want to change the essence of who I am.

It is time for us to stop all self-criticism and to accept all parts of ourselves. We can choose to learn from each part of our journey here on earth, regardless of what it shows up looking like.

Know that just as your body supports you, life supports you. Let go of the dialogue in your head that is self-judgment. Recognize that you are not alone. Whether you have been judging yourself for 5 pounds or 50, for being too shy or too extroverted, too uneducated or too smart for your own good, know that we all have dark days that cast shadows on our light.

I have chosen to forgive myself often and to spend time daily, speaking with my reflection in the mirror and thinking words of love and acceptance. I remember that I radiate beauty inside and out, because I AM light. Do that.

And then some:

1. Get a pen and paper, and ask yourself this question: "What does it feel like to be me when I am accepting myself as I am??"

2. Next, ask yourself: "When did I stop thinking that I am lovable just the way I am?" Write down your answer.

3. Make a list of the things that you are judging yourself for and the reasons that you are not feeling lovable. Even if you have been on a spiritual path for a long time, you can listen closely to your inner voice to find another opportunity for healing.

4. Meditate and send love to the areas of your life and body where you have been sending criticism and judgment.

5. Refer to the book *You Can Heal Your Life* by Louise Hay, specifically Chapter 14, which deals with the body and body image. Louise teaches how to recognize our body as a good friend with Divine Intelligence. At the end of the book, there is a section on mind-body connection that outlines ailments, possible causes, and healing affirmations. You really can heal your life. For more information on Heal Your Life® Workshops visit www.thetraining.ca and for worldwide teachers/coaches: www.healyourlifeworkshops.com

6. Continue the dialogue and make it part of your daily practice whether it is a few minutes in a journal, or a conversation in the mirror, spoken or unspoken.

CHAPTER 8

WHAT DO SHREK, A TEDDY BEAR, A GOAT AND A HORSE HAVE IN COMMON?

(Probably just this chapter, but while I have your attention let me remind you that you are so much better than your excuses.)

How many times have you wanted to start healthily moving your body, maybe go for a walk or run or take a yoga or Zumba class? Maybe boot camp or strength training is more your thing. Except, to do it ... well ... you have to do it the first time.

First-time jitters set in, and procrastination seems to be the only thing you want to add to your to-do list. You used to be good at starting something new. But now you have hit a wall. The years have made you older, the lack of movement has made you softer. Your food choices, hormones and stress level have made you as huggable as the five-foot teddy bear at Costco.

This time, starting is overwhelming and intimidating.

I have a love for hiking. Nature is my church, and in the past, I have spent a lot of time in my sanctuary. For a few years, I could not find my way back onto the trails. I had *almost* convinced myself that middle-aged people don't hike, don't strive to be fit, but instead, they settle into their Shrek-like shape and accept that they can no longer do the things they once could.

Then came a little glimmer of hope disguised as a walk around the block. Me, who not too long ago completed several distance events, including an ultramarathon and several half marathons, had to convince myself that the method to finding my way back to the trails was to start with a walk around the block. It was humbling, but that short walk built up my confidence to begin taking 15-minute walks—and then 15 minutes morphed into 20 minutes and soon I was completing 30-minute walks. All on flat terrain, all safely in my neighborhood.

And then it happened.

I went back to my old favorite hiking spot intending to trek only to the opening of the trail, and to enjoy the beauty. I parked on the side of the road and flipped open the back hatch of my vehicle to change my shoes. As I was lacing up, I could feel the excitement build in my body. It was as if it forgot that I had gained weight and it (my body) was ready to run. I could feel the adrenaline pumping through my veins. I felt like a horse on its way back to the barn—my mind was the poor cowgirl holding on for dear life.

My body remembered all of the joy, relief, tranquility, insights, tears, and accomplishments of having run this trail far too many times to count. Instead of only going to the trailhead, I went a bit further, and then a bit more, only turning back toward the vehicle because my partner (who was in his right mind) thought it would be too much for us (me) on our first time out. My partner spoke of the joy on my face, and how he had never seen me like this. He laughed and compared me to a mountain goat who is sure-footed and confident, flying over the rocks and roots with ease. I liked it. A lot.

Since then there have been many more hikes in different locations, as I live far away from my 'home church' that we visited that day. My body is still miles ahead of my mind. My body is ready to go; my mind struggles to release the beliefs that I am too old, too out of shape, too hormonal.

As I stand bent over with my hands on my knees, or sit gasping for air on a fallen log, my partner will ask me if I am okay. It reminds me that I am not the mountain goat. I respond "yes" with an edge of irritation in my voice. I want to tell him that if he wants to be okay, he will stop asking me that. Instead, I swallow my pride and know that just like anything else in life, if you want to be the expert, you have to practice consistently.

I have to practice letting go of what my mind is telling me about who I am based on what the mirror reflects. I know that my body has infinite intelligence, and that spark of life within me is saying: run, climb and jump little goat, I have got you. I'm always here for you.

Oh, how we underestimate what we can do. If we jumped out of our head, and into the infinite intelligence of the Divine spark in all of us, what could we do?

It's more than climbing physical mountains, although that part can be life-changing too. It is overcoming our perceived obstacles and trusting that the Universe is always saying, run, climb and jump my little light; I have got you. I will always be here for you.

What would you attempt to do if you could tap into the memory of who you really are, and use that momentum to leap into the life you have always wanted? Figure it out, get specific and make it happen. Do that.

And then some:

1. Get a pen and paper and divide it into three sections.
2. At the top of each section write "If I knew I could not fail, I would_____."
3. For each section keep writing in point form down the paper until you have pinpointed exactly what you want to accomplish. You don't need to know how to do it. (Just as my body remembered what to do, your infinite intelligence and Divine spark will know what to do.)
4. Believe it to be true. Now. Today. Not in the future.
5. Visualize it and connect with the *feeling* of having

exactly and precisely what you want in each area.

6. As obstacles appear, remember this chapter. They
    are merely trees, rocks or roots that are in your path.
    Go over and around them. Stay on the course. All
    you have to do is keep moving forward.

CHAPTER 9

WHO HIRED THAT VOICE IN MY HEAD?

(Um, hello, HR department? I think they may have lied on their resume.)

Our self-esteem is a combination of the positive and negative beliefs we have about ourselves. The more positive beliefs we have, the higher our self-esteem. Beliefs about one's self come from all parts of our life, starting in childhood. For more on this, refer to the Inner Child section of this book.

I can still hear my mother's voice telling me how messy I am, how I don't finish anything I start, and that I am a bull in a china shop. She was right, but that is irrelevant. I can hear my teachers saying that I have so much potential—if only I would apply myself—and that I could do better if I would stop talking and start listening. The words they were saying were accurate, but it was the feeling that I experienced when I heard these words that stuck with me. What I heard was that I was messy, a clumsy porker, lazy, and a loud mouth, with no self-control. I believed what I heard, and those thoughts became my truth.

Thoughts are like habits and become the filter through which we see ourselves. Those thoughts then influence our behavior and how we interact with other people. Simply said, when we repeat a thought enough times, it becomes a belief.

Some examples of this are people who believe they can't lose weight, who then sabotage their diet. Or people who believe they will never have enough money, and then spend everything they have. We all know someone who has a distrust of people in general and consequently is not able to cultivate meaningful relationships, romantic or otherwise. These are all a result of those long ago and often repeated thoughts that have become beliefs.

Improving the thoughts we have about ourselves will lead to improved behaviors and subsequently improved results. We don't have to wait to start that process! We can be willing to love and accept all parts of ourselves immediately. This jumpstarts change, and those repetitive thoughts that are controlling our behavior begin to lose their power over us.

When we let go of the need for approval from others, we stop comparing ourselves to other people. We must learn to stop judging, frightening, and criticizing ourselves. To do this, we need to learn the difference between our behavior and who we actually are. We are not our perceived faults. When we focus on what we do well, we will form the habit of engaging in increasingly more positive behaviors. This is who we are—pure, positive energy.

At the risk of revealing all of my deep secrets in this book, 1 will overshare—again. I have lost over 400 pounds. So that would be 115 pounds once, and 50 to 60 pounds several times. Guess what? I'm still on a diet, healthy eating plan, new lifestyle choice, or whatever I am calling it this time. I have resorted to taking severe measures to try and trick my body into giving me what I want. As I write this, I am down 60 pounds over two years and stuck. I am feeling frustrated.

Have you seen Jennifer Aniston lately? She is only a few years younger than me—why can't I look like that? Why can't I be naturally slim? Why do my fat cells hang on to me like they are clinging to a life raft in the Arctic Ocean? It's not fair! And although I joke, I write this with tears running down my face. It seems so unfair that this has been my lifelong story. On bad days, I judge myself. On most days, I feel judged by almost everyone else. That is my truth, but it is likely not factual.

In reality, some people do judge me, and that is okay. I am just not the person they relate with. The fact is that I do help a lot of people just the way I am, and they value what I have to share. Just recently, I met someone, and within 45 minutes she was in my arms sobbing as she said, "I didn't know it was okay to love myself as a bigger person." The lesson is that just because a thought has rolled around in my head long enough to become a belief, it still doesn't make it a fact or the truth.

I encourage you to examine your thoughts and beliefs. Decide if they are factual. Just because they are true for other people does not mean they have to be true for you.

Let go of what you should be, should have, should want, and should look like. 'Should' implies guilt and blame. It always makes you wrong and is a passive way of criticizing yourself. Take full responsibility for your thoughts and your subsequent actions by taking full responsibility for your life now, as it is.

How many of your beliefs—now and in the past—are even true? Probably very few of them. Think about how many of your thoughts live in the past. How much time do you spend fretting about the future?

Researchers say that 98% of what we worry about never actually happens. If you can replace those worries, thoughts and beliefs, with self-assured thoughts, you will create new experiences that reflect your new thoughts and beliefs about yourself.

How often does something happen that we perceive as negative, and then later go on to say it was one of the best things that have ever happened to us? I am sure everyone can think of at least one situation that proves this point to be true.

I was once fired from a job that was sucking the life out of me. They called it restructuring, but I knew I had been fired. I was mortified, humiliated and felt so ashamed that I didn't tell anyone other than my partner and children that I was let go. Losing my job opened doors for me in a way that allowed me to enjoy my life, and I have spent the last two decades loving what I do and making a good income doing it.

Remember that we are all the same. You will hear that a lot in this book! We all have basically the same thoughts, wants, needs, 'shoulds' and worries. This is true with samplings of people from all over the world. While improving your own thoughts and beliefs, do your part to build other people up as well. Give sincere compliments and help redirect negative thoughts and behaviors by your example.

In *A Return to Love*, Marianne Williamson states in her now-famous passage, "And as we let our own light shine, unconsciously we give other people permission to do the same." Put these words into action and shine your light, then observe what happens around you. You will be encouraged to keep on shining. After all, it is the essence of your true self.

Do that.

And then some:

1. Make a list of messages you received in your childhood so often that they became beliefs. Refer to

my examples in this chapter. Consider each one of your messages individually and decide if they are true, and more importantly if they are true for you.

2. Replace your negative messages about yourself with positive affirmations. Affirmations are personal, positive, and present tense. For more information on affirmations, visit the book resources on www.victoriajohnson.org. Using my examples, some new thoughts would be: *I lose weight easily and enjoy being healthy*, and *I easily maintain a positive cash flow each month*.

3. If you tend to have a lot of worrisome thoughts regarding the future, learn to use the self-esteem tool of visualization. For a few minutes each day, imagine, see, and connect with the *feeling* of everything always working out in the best way possible. Visualization can neutralize the past and create a future that is desirable to you.

4. Love yourself. Today. No matter what shape or size, relationship or not, career or not, financially secure or not, healthy or not. Just love yourself.

CHAPTER 10

GOD IS ALWAYS WATCHING AND WAITING TO PUNISH US
(And other lies I believed were true.)

For a long time, I thought cancer was a punishment from God, something I deserved for all of my sins and one sin in particular.

Being that I am a preacher's kid, I cut my teeth on the church pews. We were at the church four times a week and had regular devotions at least once a day at home. Overall, that was positive, as I learned ethics and values that I still hold today.

However, for as long as I remember I was told "God is Love," but like Santa, he was also keeping a naughty list. I had been taught that God is always watching and listening, sitting on his throne with a never-ending scroll recording all of my sins. I believed He even knew my sinful thoughts—which had me thinking that He must have been calling one of the saints for more ink quite frequently. Waiting for God to punish me became like playing with my jack-in-the-box toy. I would do something that was considered a sin, wait anxiously for punishment, and believe wholeheartedly that whenever something bad happened to me, it was my punishment. But, of course, I didn't let that stop me from 'sinning.'

When I got cervical cancer at twenty-two, and had it explained to me by a caring relative that it could be from being sexually promiscuous, I knew it was my punishment for what happened to me as a teenager.

When I was fifteen years old, I was on my way home from bible camp, many hours from my home, when the Greyhound bus I was traveling on made an overnight stop at the station. I knew about this ahead of time and wasn't overly concerned because it was only for five hours. What I didn't know was that the bus depot would be closed during that time.

I waited outside the station, and a few people stopped to talk to me. There was a concert that night, so traffic was heavier than usual. Two guys and two girls in a car stopped to talk to me. They were going back to the boys' parent's house for a party. "Come with us," they said. "We will drop you back off in a few hours." They seemed nice enough, clean cut, and they had two girls with them already, so I believed them and went along to their house. There was indeed a party going on, but the boys suggested that I lay down in their parents room. Their parents were out of town, and I was exhausted. I figured that was better than being downstairs at a house party so I agreed.

I could hear the party in the rest of the house and was resting, not wanting to hang out with strangers when one of the boys came in to check on me. I say boys, but they were both semi-professional junior hockey league players and in their later teens—certainly young men already. Calling them boys minimizes what happened to me, as if to say we were all the same youthful innocents. But they weren't.

The boy crawled into bed with me and then the unthinkable happened. He raped me. And he didn't stop until his older brother came in. For a moment, I thought I was safe. The brother made sure I was alright and was sweet to me. But then he was touching me, groping me, and raping me too. I lay motionless through it all. I didn't fight back, I didn't cry, and I didn't scream for help. I did what I knew to do—I emotionally detached.

I would like to say that was the end of it, but their entertainment was not over for the night. I think they wanted to get a reaction from me. They harassed me with words, and at one point defecated on a Reader's Digest magazine from their parent's ensuite and held it up to my face. I remained motionless. Eventually, they grew bored and told me to gather my things, and the older brother drove me back to the bus station. He apologized for what happened the whole way. I still felt nothing. Even when I got on that bus and went the rest of the long way home, I could feel nothing. I know now that my mind was defending itself from what I had just lived through, and I was in shock.

The following week, my mother had me share how wonderful bible camp was with the congregation. I plastered a smile on my face and kept trying to create a façade of being a good girl when I knew in my heart that I was not. The shock had worn off and the shame and guilt had settled deep within me. I knew being raped was my punishment from God for already being sexually active in my past. God had been watching, and He had punished me.

I have been terrified to share this story. I kept my mouth shut and knew I would never tell because then I would have to admit to the shame of having made stupid choices, being a sexual sinner, letting my loved ones down, and everyone would know that God had punished me, and I deserved what I got. Or, at least, that was what I thought about myself and what happened that night.

Fast forward seven years, and with my diagnosis, it all came rushing back. I had cancer in what was a strictly female area—my cervix. This was my punishment for letting myself be raped, becoming promiscuous in my later teen years, and for having two different baby daddies to my young sons. God was still watching me and waiting to punish me. Once again, I felt the deep shame of what had happened, of what *I* had done. I had got in that car, I had kept quiet, I had *let* those boys rape me, and I believed that I deserved to be punished with the type of cancer you get from being a slutty teenager. And I endured my punishment alone.

67

I had multiple surgeries and was deemed cancer free and told that I could go back to life as per usual. Life per usual was a colossal mess, and the only skills I had honed to perfection were how to keep silent and how to bury shame.

When I went through a spiritual awakening in my thirties, examining that night was one of the last things I wanted to do. It was painful to revisit and felt so much easier to bury it, but as I learned about the mind-body connection, I knew I couldn't hide from what happened anymore. I had to bring it out into the light. I realized that what I had been taught about God watching and waiting to punish us for our sins was not something I actually believed in.

So then, I had to really think about why this happened to me and why I got cancer. I came to realize that there wasn't a why. It was a moment in my life that had happened. I had the choice to remain a victim of that night or to allow myself to heal. I won't sugar coat it—it has been hard work to heal the deeply buried shame and terror I felt that night. But in that healing was the great gift of knowing that my cancer wasn't a punishment from God but was, in my opinion, directly related to the shame I had buried deep within myself all those years. That shame had manifested as cancer in my body, which made so much more sense to me. My hidden memories needed to be released from somewhere, and they released themselves in the form of cancer in my reproductive system. Once I could release the shame and guilt and fear, I could find peace in all that had happened to me. I could find gratitude in having gotten pregnant young, so that I could be a mom before my mind/body created this cancer and took that from me. I could find gratitude in being able to see that my sexual activity did not make me a sinner, and that God is love and I was loved no matter what. It took me longer to find resolution for the night I was raped. But as I became a life coach and began to work with women who had similar stories, I found gratitude for my deep understanding of what they had been through, and that knowledge helped me to help them.

Even in the face of our darkest nightmares, our job is to know that the Universe always has our back, no matter what. Let go of the shame. Do that.

And then some:

1. Please know that you do not deserve any trauma that comes your way. Whatever challenges life has presented, you have found your way through them. Make a list of all the significant challenges that you have overcome, and spend some time celebrating how resourceful and strong you are.

2. Accept that you are not your past, and at no point does it define you. As you review the above list, do you find yourself believing that is who you are? Just because you have been sick in the past, it does not make you sickly now. Just because you have cheated/

been cheated on in the past, it does not make you less deserving of a healthy relationship now. You are who you are today. What do you think you deserve? Write it down.

3. When you compare your answers from questions 1 and 2, is there a significant contrast between the two? Are they similar? Spend some time in meditation and review each point.

4. To heal from what has happened to you in the past, pay attention to which parts of yourself you have not forgiven. As you think of these things, close your eyes, and place your hand on your heart's center, and send love to yourself. Be willing to forgive yourself for what you perceive to be your part in any of the trauma from which you desire to be healed.

5. Stop concerning yourself with what other people think of you. It doesn't matter. This is your life. No one knows what it is like to be you. And after five decades on this earth, let me assure you of two things:

   a. If people are judging you, it is out of their own fear.

   b. Most people are so wrapped up in their own lives that they don't spend a great deal of time worrying about what you are doing wrong in yours. If they do? Dump them. Period. Relative or not.

6. Find a confidante to help you through both the good times and the bad. Make a deal that you can tell each other anything without judgment from the other—no matter what.

7. Expose the shame and let go of the blame. If you can talk to your confidante about the secrets you carry as shame, do that. If you don't feel like you can do that, then write a letter to yourself. Lay it all out—all of the feelings, memories, and subsequent consequences. When it is all out on paper, keep it stashed away somewhere and read it over and over until you can read the letter out loud without emotion. Then you will know that you have exposed the darkness to the light and that it no longer has any power over you.

8. Forgive yourself, forgive others. Repeat often.

CHAPTER 11

A LIFE WITHOUT LIMITS

*(There is no comfort in
the comfort zone.)*

Let's face it, we all want at least some degree of health, wealth and happiness. Often, we just don't know what order or to what degree we want them in! Additionally, we don't know how to get from where we are now to the next level we would like to achieve.

It seems we can navigate through life making sure we are never too dull or too bright. We move forward only when we can clearly see that it is safe to do so and that everyone else is doing it. There are people in front of us, and people behind us, and most of us are tucked safely into the middle maintaining the status quo. Not too healthy, not too unhealthy. Not too rich, not too poor. Not too happy, not too unhappy.

Mediocrity can be very comfortable for many people. Judgment there is kept to a minimum. If that is where you are and where you want to stay, there is no shame in that. For those of us who have a deep instinctual belief that there is more available for us—there is no comfort in the comfort zone!

Mediocrity becomes a place where we feel inadequate and a million miles away from where we are destined to be. We have a great life … a life many people would only dream of. Somehow, it is not enough even though logically it appears to be, especially when we compare ourselves to those less fortunate in the world. Insert self-induced guilt here!

In order to avoid exhaustion and frustration in the process, we must obtain a humility that allows service to resonate in all that we say and do. 'How may I serve' must become our mantra. When we concern ourselves with the perceived limitations and judgment of others, or rely on the praise and support of others, we give away our power. Our success or lack thereof begins to hinge on people and events outside of ourselves. We lose our authenticity in order to maintain that delicate balance of service to that which is outside of our true nature.

This is when we become firmly planted in the comfort zone. We lose touch with our inner guidance, and instead use the opinions, approval and judgments of others as our compass for the road ahead. Everyday things become more difficult, we become more and more tired, we question our progress, our purpose and our dreams. We are not living the life we know is there for us and eventually our health pays the price.

My client Val has consented to the sharing of her story. We started our coaching relationship when she began experiencing stress at work. Val felt that she couldn't do anything right and that the upper management did not approve of her. She was responsible for seventy employees and depended on the support of the upper management, which wasn't forthcoming. She shared that she felt like a fraud and a failure when she smiled all day and pretended to be happy. Val had considered leaving the job, but she knew that she was a good manager and that she was appreciated and supported by those under her.

During the past year, Val had been experiencing physical pain in her neck. Thinking it was glandular or an ear infection, she saw doctor after doctor. Eventually she was diagnosed with TMJ—a condition where the jaw joint is inflamed often as a result of clutching the teeth and face tightly due to stress.

Val realized that she had to find a way to keep the job she loved, and to accept that she may never be supported by upper management. Through visualization and meditation, she was able to change her thoughts and to relax to release the negative emotions. She realized that the management style of her leaders was a reflection of how they manage, not about how she leads her people. Over time, she developed healthier ways to deal with stress, and the TMJ subsided. Val's takeaway from our sessions was that when she changes who she is for other people, it shows up as dis-ease in the body. When she does what is in her nature, integrity and ethics, her whole body relaxes, and she is more balanced in mind, body and spirit. Val realized that she was not comfortable with mediocrity and found a way to stay within her current situation while still being true to herself.

The key to sustaining forward motion is to seek alignment in our mind, body and spirit. Taking care of our whole self will result in an energy vibration that will allow everything in our life to coordinate effortlessly at exactly the right time. Remember that we are all responsible for our own lives, and we cannot expect other people to modify their behavior. The Law of Attraction will respond to our physical thoughts and inner beliefs. In all things, whether they are negative or positive, we are attracting them into our life in response to the attention we are giving them.

By the very virtue of your emotional/spiritual vibration, you are attracting your future. I encourage you to consistently offer thoughts and actions that take you beyond your comfort zone. By using visualization, you will move easily into the life you dream of for yourself. As long as you are looking forward with optimism, seeing the best in every situation, ultimately 'the best' will become your new normal, your new comfort zone. Only then can the process repeat itself, lifting you to an even greater feeling of wholeness with each repetition. You deserve all the health, wealth, and happiness you can imagine. Learn to live a life without limits. Do that.

And then some:

1. Make it a point to talk and think like people you admire. Examine who you are surrounding yourself with because that often dictates how you will speak, think and behave. If you don't have those people within your reach, instead reach for books, podcasts and videos of the people you admire.

2. When you change your thoughts, you change your life. Think about which thoughts got you to your current place, and think about what you would like to change. Practice changing the small things first, and then move on to the larger things in your life.

3. Focus on your passion. As your body is firing up those feel-good endorphins, your health will respond accordingly.

4. Drop your fear of failure. Accept that failing is part of your success, and welcome it when it shows up. Many of us are scared to fail. We don't believe we have what it takes to make things happen. Embrace failure and you will find success soon after.

5. Let go of what you perceive other people think of you. Most likely they are not thinking of you at all, and if they are, they are looking at you through the lens of their own perspective. Your responsibility is to be true to yourself.

6. Check in with your physical health regularly. What areas are you experiencing both physical and mental

dis-ease? Speak to a coach or counselor to find the root of the dis-ease and your body will thank you with vibrant health and energy.

CHAPTER 12

MIRROR, MIRROR ON THE WALL
(Am I the most stressed of them all?)

Self-reflection is definitely not for the faint of heart. Stress causes upheaval in all areas of our life, and when we are under stress, taking a good look at ourselves is not on the top of our priority list—even though it potentially has the power to get us back on track. As a society, we are so busy just trying to live life that we often fail to take the time out to examine why we do the things we do.

We live in a society in which we wear work-stress like a badge of honor. Sometimes it appears people are trying to be over-stressed! Do you think about work while you eat, check your email in the bathroom, dream of work at night, and talk about your work to anyone who will (appear to) listen? Maybe you are the opposite, nose to the grindstone all day, and lips to the wine glass all night.

Another badge we wear with honor is that of being busy and rushing from place to place and task to task. This goes hand in hand with being stressed. It's possible that we don't even know if we are bragging or complaining about how busy we are.

I remember the day that I was determined to fit in an awards ceremony at my granddaughter's school. I got up that morning and went to a volunteer breakfast, stopped off at the bank, ran an errand for business, met with a client for a planning meeting, and then came home for a conference call regarding my website. As I was finishing that, my son popped in and asked how I was—I replied that I was busy and stressed to the max. I was excited to see him, yet we rushed through our visit as we stood by the stove eating lunch straight from the pan together. I glanced at the clock. It was 15 minutes until my granddaughter's (from my other son) awards assembly.

My son left, and I quickly pulled on my high-heeled snow boots (yes, there is such a thing) and headed out to my vehicle. As I got there, I realized that I did not have my keys. My business cell phone rang, and I answered while running around the house looking for my keys. Then it happened—my wet boots slipped on the hardwood floor. I landed on my belly, sliding like a bowling ball down the lane with the walls acting as bumper pads. I caught my breath and kept talking to the client like nothing had happened when really I wanted to cry out in pain.

After booking the client for an appointment, I hung up and lay there for a few moments. I determined that nothing but my pride was hurt so I got up and resumed my frenzied hunt for the keys. That is when it happened again—this time even quicker. Suddenly I was on the floor on my hands and knees in so much pain I was sure

I had seriously hurt myself. I scooted on my backside to a chair and just sat there for a while before pulling myself up. "Okay Universe," I said. "You have my attention—what is the message?" I knew the message. I had heard it before ... *there is no award for being the most busy or the most stressed. Slow down. Enjoy the moments of your life.*

In order to see how stress is impacting your life, self-reflection is a good place to start. If you are not familiar with self-reflection, here is a brief outline to get you started.

Self-reflection is a way to look at your life, examine your actions, and ask yourself questions that will help you understand more about yourself. It is easy to only think of your thoughts and motivations on the surface level. Self-reflection is an opportunity to go much deeper—to understand yourself and your feelings entirely. This will help you gain a better understanding of where you might be going off your desired path and give you clarity on different areas that you could improve in your day-to-day life.

Looking inside at your own behaviors and habits will be beneficial to many areas of your life, from weight loss to improving mental health conditions like insomnia and anxiety, which brings us back to what we are looking at in this chapter. Stress. I always say that food and stress can kill you; let's take a closer look at the impacts of stress on your body.

Stress may be the driving force behind illness in your body. It affects all systems of the body, including respiratory, cardiovascular, digestive, muscular, reproductive, and the immune system. It causes high blood pressure, heart problems, diabetes and less obvious dis-eases such as negative thoughts, suppressed feelings and sabotaging behaviors.

I once (okay, many times, but one time in particular) felt extreme stress for a long period of time. My physical and emotional states of being were both greatly impacted. I owned a business, and unbeknownst to me, my staff and clients were taken to a room in the back of the building and held against their will. I heard some commotion and went to investigate, only to discover a man with a knife demanding money. The situation was resolved and everyone was safe. That night, I did everything that I knew to do. I called the staff and the clients and asked if they were okay. I went back to the place of business and mentally cleared the energy of each room. I even took some time to send positive energy and prayer to the robber. I imagined how desperate he must have been to have robbed us in the middle of the day.

I thought that the emotions and the physical fear would pass, but instead they grew stronger. I experienced extreme headaches and seemed to gain weight while I slept. I was exhausted to the point of not being physically able to stay awake for more than a few hours at a time. I was too tired to exercise and the pain in my body grew as

81

my muscles longed for physical activity. The emotional impact was staggering as well. I became suspicious of people walking down the street. If I witnessed a lone man walk into a business, I wanted to stop and go in to make sure everything was okay. Almost every night I would dream of the robbery. Each dream ended with me physically attacking the robber.

Eventually I started seeing a psychologist and was diagnosed with PTSD. She concluded that even though the situation of the robbery turned out safely, it triggered stressful events from my childhood and young adult life where I did not feel safe. The body and mind remembered the stress and returned to it. This time I couldn't repress the emotions or the physical consequences, and they took over. I was just along for the ride. My therapist and I went through a series of sessions where we reflected back to the times when I was deeply stressed, and I took the time and painful effort to examine those feelings. It was then that I was able to release the stress, and eventually get back to my usual self—but without all of the old-self stuff hidden below the surface.

Examining stressors sounds like a good idea but is not something that most people want to make the time and effort to do. In my attempt to simplify the process and motivate you, I have narrowed the scope of this chapter to identify how stress may show up in your life both personally and professionally, followed by questions to ask yourself in the self-reflection process. You won't only be uncovering painful experiences and trauma. You will also be uncovering your successes and things that have relieved stress for you in the past. Both of these self-reflection techniques will help you in your self-improvement journey.

According to the US Center for Disease Control/National Institute for Occupational Safety and Health, the workplace is the number one cause of stress in our lives. But work stress is not something to brag about.

I live in an area where there are many trades workers who work long shifts several days in a row and will then have a few consecutive days off. The stress of the work is so great that often people turn to consumption of drugs and alcohol between sets of working days. This snowballs into financial and relationship stress because they are often neglecting parts of their life in order to find relief. This is an example of physical, mental, and emotional stress and how it impacts all areas of life—not just the primary source of stress. The same principle applies if the stress begins at home, in romantic or platonic relationships, is financial, or is caused by a traumatic event. Stress cannot be isolated; it impacts our whole being.

When we become stressed, we have a tendency to hide, overlook, or ignore our feelings and become reclusive. Having friends in our life, even in small numbers, is much more important for our health and wellness than most of us realize. Genuine friends are those that we can talk to about anything and everything. They listen and encourage us to be our best self.

If you find that you don't have close friends, then it might be time to look at yourself to determine why that is. Again, using self-reflection helps you get to the root of why you are withdrawing from friendships, just as it helps you to set healthy boundaries in your work life.

Have you found yourself becoming less patient? Patience is a virtue, and not everyone has it. But don't use that as an excuse. Lack of patience is a sign that you need to look within and find out what is driving you to lose your mind in a traffic jam or cause a scene in the check-out line. Confession: I do the latter quite frequently. Patience is not something everyone has an easy time practicing. I have been practicing it a lot.

Lack of patience often indicates that your stress and anxiety are on the rise, making even menial tasks like standing in line feel like a disrespectful waste of your time. If you are low on patience, cultivate friendships with people who respect your time and have mastered the art of making a long story short! To reduce stress, consider adding meditation into your life.

Stress is a breeding ground for unhealthy habits, which are another sign that it is time for some self-improvement practices. Unhealthy habits include anything that you feel is hurting your physical or mental health, from substance abuse and food addiction to procrastinating or not getting enough sleep or physical activity. Many people find that when they start self-reflecting and working on themselves, unhealthy habits self-correct. Self-care has become a catchphrase in the self-help industry, but it is for a good reason. If you are not taking care of yourself, sooner or later stress will catch up and *force* you to add self-care into your life.

Do you find that you are losing interest in things you used to enjoy? This can be a sign of depression, but it's also a sign that you are in need of a little self-love. Loss of interest in life causes you to lack the motivation you need to better yourself. Loss of interest is a sign that your life is missing something—passion. Passion for your dreams, passion for life, passion for people and things around you.

Are you paying attention to maintaining a friendship with the person you see in the mirror? Have self-criticism and self-judgment taken over to control your thoughts? It doesn't take much of a stretch for these two sneaky saboteurs to turn negative thoughts into self-loathing. It is much easier to find things to loathe about other people than it is to look at our own shortcomings. The people that irritate us the most are the people who are mirroring what we don't like about ourselves. It is much easier to be triggered by other people than it is to catch ourselves in the despicable act we are judging someone else for.

Self-reflection is not self-focused. I have a friend who is extremely self-focused. She can make everything about herself and is a master at one-upping any experience that

I have had. She always has a story to tell that is more bizarre, funny or sweet than the story I just told. When I share that I have read a book that I am excited about, then OMG, she read it too and has researched the author and pre-ordered the sequel. When I tell the story about how I once skied off the side of a mountain, wrapped myself around a tree and had to be rescued by the ski-patrol, OMG, that happened to her too—in Switzerland—with Shania Twain, and they went back to her villa there afterward for tea. Really.

True story. A different friend of mine was telling me a story about her friend who showed these characteristics and I said, OMG, I have a friend like that too. Really. Self-reflection helped me to see that the reason that type of behavior was triggering me so much with my friend was that it was a part of myself that I didn't want to look at. I react with physical and emotional stress whenever I am around the 'skiing with Shania' friend because I don't feel like I am heard or that my sharing is validated. When I realized that I was doing that to other people as well, I was able to grow and make changes. I let go of friendships that were causing me stress, and I learned how to be a better friend in the process.

Does external validation drive you? This is another key stress indicator. It is also a ticking time bomb. When we look for someone or something outside of ourselves to measure our worth, we not only do ourselves a great disservice, we also disrespect ourselves. Add to that, the variable that we have no control in how, when or why others will bless us with their validation and we become as fragile as a bird with broken wings.

Self-reflection helps us to identify where we are saying yes to other people, and no to ourselves. We can see where we can do less, subsequently creating more time for ourselves. We can see where we can pull the brake and get off the crazy train of external validation and back on a more peaceful track that is headed in the direction we want to be going.

If you truly desire to minimize the stress in your life, practice self-reflection by answering these questions:

What do I complain about the most? How is my complaining contaminating other areas of my life? What are my goals? Are my current actions helping me move toward those goals? What do I repetitively do that could be done in a healthier way? What is it that I struggle with the most? How are my personal relationships? When I think back over my day, how can I change my reaction regarding the things that cause me stress? What am I struggling with the most? What can I do differently—no matter how big or how small—that will positively impact my life? Do that.

And then some:

1. Write in a journal daily. Journaling is one of the best tools for self-improvement in general, but especially

when you are striving to become more self-aware. There is a journal outline for you in the book resources section at www.victoriajohnson.org. You can use the journal when asking yourself the above questions and also to journal daily about your thoughts and feelings. Try to turn this into a regular practice.

2. Be honest with yourself. Self-reflection is not something you need to share with anyone else. By keeping it personal and private, you can be honest and dig deep into your emotions. You can identify where you might need some attention. It is essential that you are honest with yourself! If you are not honest with yourself, you will not make sustainable changes.

3. Since self-reflection is something you will do over a long period of time, keep checking in with yourself. If you first wrote in your journal a month ago, now is a good time to check in and answer the same questions you answered before. This process will allow you to see how far you have come and which areas still need attention. Celebrate your successes.

4. Make self-reflection a daily practice. When possible, practice near the end of your day, and preferably in your journal. Not only is the self-reflection valuable, it also puts you in a positive mind frame for the following day. The purpose of this practice is to look at not only what happens in your life, but also to

turn your attention to what you desire and what actions are needed.

5. Write a letter to yourself describing what your life would look like if you were not in a chronic state of stress. For example, describe your ideal workday, relationships, health, spiritual practice and so on.

6. Re-read the first sentence of this chapter. It makes more sense now, doesn't it?

SECTION THREE

YOUR RELATIONSHIPS:
THEY SAY A LOT ABOUT YOU

CHAPTER 13

FAMILY DYNAMICS

*(Zero to crazy in 1.2 seconds—
these people have you dialed in.)*

Sometimes writing is really hard. I mean really hard. There are times I feel like I would like to get a job doing heavy intense labor to avoid the labor of delivering this book. This section on relationships has been the hardest. I have had to go deep inside myself, dig up my feelings, and then be brave enough to share them with you. I have had to consider the family and friends who may be shocked or hurt about what I am writing, and then do it anyway. In the final six weeks of writing the first draft of this book, I developed multiple minor infections and gained twenty pounds. I lost my zest for adventure and became my most introverted self. I would have happily locked myself in the bedroom and stayed there day and night, squeezing out a few sentences between naps and 90's sitcoms. When taking the road less traveled, that is not an option.

As you read through this section on relationships, please understand that the intention is to help you. I speak my truth to help you recognize your truth. We are all the same.

We might not all go through the same circumstances, but we have the same feelings, the same fears, and we have experienced both failed and successful relationships. Every relationship we have teaches us something. When we build positive relationships with others, we feel happier, supported, supportive, connected and more fulfilled. They are part of our very being, and no matter what our ego tells us, healthy primary relationships are as necessary for happiness as breathing is to life.

Family dynamics are in all cultures; no one is exempt. We all have our own version of what our truth is. Those truths are based on a belief system that we formed early on in life and then experienced their reoccurrence in both self-created and uncontrollable situations. The foundation on which I learned to interact with other people was established early on. I wasn't one of those children who felt special or chosen when they were adopted. I felt abandoned, left, not good enough, defective, unlovable, alone, and for lack of a more sophisticated word—bad. (As in, I must have been such a bad baby that my biological family just couldn't handle me.) I never placed the blame or responsibility outward; I internalized it as something that was my fault.

I had hints of anger regarding my adoption when I wrote about it earlier in this book, but it was nothing like the no-holds-barred questioning of the adoption system that has been bubbling inside of me over the last few weeks. There is enough thought going on between my ears to write a second book. All of this thought is questioning the system. What if giving up a child isn't selfless; what if it is selfish? What if the whole system is causing far more harm than good? What if none of the babies adopted at birth are actually chosen? I mean, how can they be? They are not even born yet.

A general theme runs through all of these underlying thoughts—be careful with your loved ones; they are precious and fragile. They can be shattered by your words and destroyed by your actions. As adults we can work through these hurts and grieve for the hurt child, but as a child we have no choice but to learn to exist by coping.

You are loved for who you are. Except when you are not. In a world full of muddy relationships, a strained relationship between parents and children is the most polluted. It's not just about adoption; in fact, that is the very rare minority. Think of all the biological children—perhaps yourself included—who have felt rejected by their parents or family members. Think of all of the lovers, partners, spouses, and friends who have felt the first sting of rejection and questioned their own worth. Even the workplace is a breeding ground for negative emotions. My point is, we have all experienced rejection, we have all rejected another person, we have all been treated unfairly and we have all treated someone else disrespectfully. That is why this chapter and section is applicable to everyone. We are going there—examining relationships—and in this chapter, specifically family relationships.

Healthy family relationships are based on love and trust, but they also consist of giving and receiving. Ideally, both can be done without reservations, conditions, or expectations. If you choose to give to your family either by doing, being, or monetarily, what is your payoff? Do you feel like you need recognition? Is it a pat on the back, or a thank you? Or do you give because you are trying to buy love (with time, doing, being something to someone, or money) or to fill your own ego about how wonderful you are?

Sometimes we just want to give—without anxiety or barriers. I had an amazing opportunity to do that a few years back. I have examined the situation from all the angles I can think of, and I am confident that I was just giving because I could give. I may be too close to the situation; you are welcome to form your own opinion. It certainly had an impact on my family dynamic, and my goal in sharing this story is to stimulate your thoughts as to the dynamic of your family.

This story is about my birth family. We were reunited when I was twenty-three, and I was thrilled to discover that my parents were married, and in addition to my three older half-sisters, I also had three blood-related siblings. As an aside, this is not to dismiss anyone in my adoptive family; I am simply choosing to share this experience as it was a life changer for me.

In the early days of the reunion, everything was lovely and frankly we could have had our own feel-good movie.

That didn't last long. Over the next few years, I became estranged from my birth family. I was going to be gracious and tell you that this was in large part due to my choices, but I'm not really sure about that. Maybe sometimes people just are the way they are and twenty-three years one way or the other doesn't change that. I cut off all contact with my birth mother after several experiences had left me feeling rejected all over again. I don't think that is a feeling reserved only for adopted and reunited children. Many adult children go through this rejection day after day, week after week. My choice was to end the relationship. Luckily, I had an adoptive mother who loved me every day, so I didn't much feel like spending a lot of time trying to earn the love of the mother who left me as an infant. Or so I told myself.

A few years later my youngest sister became ill and needed a kidney. We spoke on the phone, and without hesitation I agreed to be tested to see if I was a match as a donor. She and I had a complicated past, but we had moved through it. Charlotte's children were five and nine at the time, and I wanted to be part of her recovery. The affection of my birth mother increased after I'd agreed to be tested, and I began hearing the familiar dialogue of how much she had always loved me. I was helping her golden child, so I was very easy to love at that time.

In our family relationships, the line between perception and reality is blurred. My rejected self wants to take many things personally. I still desire acceptance and inclusion with my birth family, but I am at peace being on the outside of the inner circle. The shift is that now I have chosen to be there and hold no emotional attachment to the reality of the situation. Or so I tell myself.

Family relationships can be difficult—if not impossible—to navigate. To this day, I believe that my birth mother believes that she loves me. And, to this day, I don't believe she loves me like a mother loves a child. Maybe it has nothing to do with me, and maybe she still struggles to forgive herself for the 'gift' we call adoption. I don't know; I just know it is complicated.

My kidney was placed in my sister, and my birth mother often called and spoke lovingly to me, expressing her gratitude at having me in her life. Her affection began to run thin after the transplant when I voiced my concerns over Charlotte's lifestyle choices. A few weeks later Charlotte passed away, and after the flurry of activity regarding the funeral and custody of her children, communication gradually lessened again. I am not blaming my birth mother for that. I am simply shining a light on the fact that sometimes there are family dynamics that are so complicated, so convoluted, and so complex, that abstinence is the best alternative.

Although I do not have frequent contact with my birth family, I remind myself that I am capable of having healthy family relationships. I have a reciprocal relationship with my adoptive family. Giving, accepting, receiving, and loving and doing are as habitual and easy as brushing our teeth in the morning. We take those actions without thinking. In both my birth and adoptive families, I am learning to accept the things that make us different. As I love and accept myself as I am, I can love and accept each other family member as they are.

Once I learned to let go of the labels I had given myself in childhood, I was able to more clearly see who I am. Instead of being not good enough, defective, unlovable, alone, and bad, I became willing to see the side of myself that was the exact opposite. I began to believe that I was good enough just because I exist, perfectly me, surrounded by people who are the same, and above all, I was able to drop the belief that I was bad.

And that, dear reader, is the objective of the chapters in this section. Hell, let's be honest. It is the point of this entire book. You can change your thoughts, which changes your beliefs, which changes how you see the world, and changes your relationships, including your relationship with self. You can begin to see the world as a safe place to have, give, receive, to set boundaries, and to respect the boundaries of others. Do that.

And then some:

One of the most profound experiences we can have in our lives is the connection we have with other human beings. Positive and supportive relationships help us to feel healthier, happier, and more satisfied with our lives.

Here are a few tips to help you to develop more positive and healthy relationships in all areas of your life.

1.   Do your personal growth work. It is never-ending. I often have people tell me they have done all of their personal growth and they don't need anymore. The truth is, we are not done until we are dead. And even after that—who knows! Commit to a daily practice. Whether it is five minutes or an hour, be sure to be nurturing your own growth daily. For ideas on how to do this go to the resources on www.victoriajohnson.org.

2.   Learn to accept that all relationships are different. We all see the reality of a situation a little differently than others. Imagine that you are seeing the world through tinted sunglasses. Everyone has a little different tint in their shades. You can choose to change your glasses and look at things from a different perspective.

3.   Listen effectively. Listening is a crucial skill in avoiding misunderstanding and helping the other person feel supported and valued. Active listening requires checking in to our own interpretation and reflecting back the message to the speaker before we add our own thoughts and opinions. This is crucial in conversations where stress levels are elevated.

4.   Block off periods of time to nurture your relationship with self and others. When you make time for yourself and others, you send out the message: "You

are important to me." Be present. Try to meet without preconceived notions or old emotions with you. For example, you may be thinking, *I am having lunch with Mom on Friday and I am going to have to spend the whole hour listening to her complain about every little ache and pain she has. She is always having a pity party about getting older. If she would just get more exercise, she would feel better.* When you meet with her, you have already set the tone and will likely get exactly what you are expecting. Once again, strive to live in the present moment.

5. Learn to give and take feedback. When asked, constructive feedback can build stronger relationships. When you are open to receiving feedback from others, their opinion on how you present yourself in relationships provides you with a different perspective on your role in the relationship and is yet another opportunity for personal growth. I admit, it is scary to go there, but the benefit can outweigh the risk. Be sure that the person you are seeking feedback from is someone whom you trust.

6. Learn to trust more. Trust is important in any relationship and especially with primary relationships—family or romantic. Trust can be more difficult when you have been hurt, and when someone has repeatedly hurt you, it is wise to trust your instincts more than the other person's words. In general, love and trust become the foundation of all of our relationships. As far back as I can

remember I have been told that trust has to be earned. Does it? Spend time meditating and contemplating your thoughts on love and trust. You will be more aware of your choices and confident in your beliefs when you form your own opinion.

7. Ask yourself what you need to let go of. Listen closely for the wisdom from your inner voice.

CHAPTER 14

IT'S NOT THE RIGHT THING TO DO IF IT'S NOT RIGHT FOR YOU

(Self-sacrifice all dressed up in its Sunday finest.)

Often in our relationships we think we're doing the right thing by doing what someone else wants. We call it compromise, and we stuff our feelings down in the hope of making another person happy. In fact, compromise is something else entirely. Sacrificing ourselves for a relationship is actually sacrificing the long-term success of the relationship.

You know those times when you really don't want something, and you go along with it anyway or forgo your success in order to make other people feel comfortable? Yes? Me too. Just keep reading.

When we do what we think is expected of us or try to live up to what we think are society's expectations, we often end up miserable, beating ourselves up with harmful self-talk, and negatively impacting our lives for years or even decades. When we were teenagers, they called it peer pressure and acted like it was a phase we were going through. Hell, no! As adults it is still going strong.

Mavis, a coaching client of mine just experienced this and she is far past her teenage years. She has consented to me sharing her story with you. Mavis is a travel agent who works as a contractor to a major travel agency. She is a mentor for other agents in her region and is often called upon by the company to train their new hires. This provides her with an extra form of revenue and is a crucial part of her annual income. Even though there are no territories, it is widely expected that there be a professional courtesy between agents.

Mavis lives in a small city on the eastern side of the United States, and the annual trade show for her industry was being held in a large city on the west coast. It was both an educational and networking opportunity, so she registered early and planned to attend. The person who held Mavis's position in the west was resistant to having Mavis networking at the event, because the western representative was struggling in both sales, and in training new hires. Mavis then began to feel guilty about her own success and began to believe that her attendance would negatively impact the western mentor in her efforts to form meaningful relationships. She was torn. She really wanted to attend but was uncomfortable because she felt unwanted, and she eventually bowed out of the event. The head office manager of the travel agency complimented her on her generosity and thoughtfulness, and Mavis felt peaceful about her decision.

The weekend of the event came. Each day Mavis was aware of what she was missing out on, and she cried her eyes out for three days straight. The tears were coming from frustration, and she questioned and cursed her decision even though it was far too late to do anything about it.

Our Monday morning coaching session started like this. Mavis was crying and furious with herself. She stated, "I can't decide where to start! I'm angry, frustrated, pissed off at the world, pissed off at myself, want to slap myself in the forehead and scream how could you be so stupid! All weekend I kept trying to convince myself I did the right thing, but the truth is I missed out on a great opportunity. I kept scolding myself about having limited thinking and telling myself to be generous, be gracious, but the truth is that I really was doing the right thing— but it was the right thing for *someone else*, not for myself. I cared more about what other people thought of me than I did my own success. I wanted to be liked and threw myself under the bus to make it happen."

Upon discussion we uncovered that Mavis had spent many years of her life being a high achiever and subsequently being chastised for shining too bright or having too big of a personality. Because she was sensitive and afraid of making someone else feel bad, she backed away from an opportunity. She knew she was not wanted there, and the thought of dimming her light and opening herself up to criticism and rejection fed a fear in her that ultimately was the tipping point in her decision to not attend. Mavis was afraid that if she attended the trade show and the other sales rep for the agency did not end up having a strong year, she would be blamed. And there it was, the root cause, the feelings of being judged by her equals and superiors in the agency, the feelings of not deserving to be successful when others were struggling, and the feelings of her core personality traits being rejected for being too bright or too powerful. This hurt was a pattern in her life and it ran deep.

Mavis went on to share how as a nineteen-year-old she fell in love and became pregnant. In her excitement she went on to accept the proposal of the baby's father and they began to plan the wedding for three months later. A month before the wedding she realized that she was making a mistake by rushing into marriage. She spoke to her parents who were paying for the wedding and was told that it was too late to change her mind. The invitations had all been sent out and people had made arrangements to travel. She was told that she had to be responsible and get married and live with the consequences of her actions. Just like the weekend of the trade show, she didn't want to cause problems for others, and so she agreed to go forward with the wedding. Even back then, she had thrown herself under the bus to make other people happy. The marriage dissolved within a few months and she was left feeling even more morose for going along with the pretense of doing the right thing.

At the root of these situations is fear. Fear of being blamed and fear of feeling yet another rejection. Over her lifetime Mavis had developed a pattern where she avoided putting herself in situations where she could be rejected, judged or criticized. She made important decisions about her life from fear, rather than from her love, strength and power without even realizing that she was doing it. She was so conditioned to people telling her how strong and powerful she was that she didn't realize the root of her desire for approval was fear.

What Mavis is learning in our coaching sessions is that her happiness matters and she deserves to have everything she wants. It doesn't make her insensitive, overbearing, selfish or indicate that she shines too bright or has too big of a personality when she makes herself a priority and listens to her inner voice. She is learning to make decisions from a true place of love, not decisions that appear loving but are actually based in fear of rejection or blame. She still struggles with the uncomfortable feelings that come with people telling her that she accomplishes more in a day than most do in a month, but she is learning to let go of that undeserved guilt. She is willing to learn to accept that her bright light does not dim anyone else's. Mavis is discovering how to be true to herself and move through her feelings around worthiness. And it is beautiful.

Another lesson in Mavis's experience is self-sacrifice. I'm not talking about compromise. I am talking about laying down on the pavement on a well-known bus route. And waiting. Why do we do this? Part of it is because it feels good in the moment. We live in a society where people are applauded and celebrated for doing the right thing or the nice thing. What if we said no? Or more expressively, what if we said f#*k that?

Referring back to the first chapter of this section where I was talking about my adoption and the feelings that surrounded it, what if my birth mother stood up for herself and made a different decision? What if she said no, I am not surrendering my child even though someone told me it is the right thing to do? There were no addicts involved, no danger, no reason at all that the community my mother was involved in couldn't have helped her to raise me. After all, don't they also say it takes a village to raise a child? Instead, she was counseled to do the right thing, the gracious thing, and give me away with a request that I be placed in a nice Christian home. Really? I have told you of some of the consequences that decision had on my life, but I can't even imagine the impact that sacrifice had on her life. She was haunted for decades, wondering what had become of me, and longing for the child she nurtured and loved.

Once again, sacrificing yourself may seem noble in the moment, but ultimately, it's not the right thing to do if it's not right for you.

There has been healing in Mavis's and my birth mother's life. They have learned to listen to the voice inside of them that lets them know that it is okay to feel the fear and stay with it. They don't have to push it away or mask it, because by really staying with the fear and letting it run through all of the emotions that come with it, they become free to make decisions from a healthy place of self-love. Do that.

And then some:

1. Get Susan Jeffers book, *Feel the Fear and Do It Anyway*. Read it!

2. The word sacrifice is defined by most as giving up something that is valuable to please someone else or to meet someone else's needs over our own. It is no-win situation. We can't go back in time and make a different decision. What we can do is bring awareness to our past through self-examination in order to identify the fear and break the pattern for the future.

3. The present moment is the only moment we have, so we can strive to get to a place of peace now, even if it is years after the sacrifice was made. Allow yourself to feel the emotions that were brought up when you "did the right thing." Was there anger, resentment, or shame? Just sit with that feeling. Feel it in your body, and don't allow your thoughts to give you a logical solution to make the feelings go away. Just sit in it. After a while, you will feel the unpleasant feelings subside, and you will begin to

have peace. Repeat this process as often as you need to until you have completely let go of the sacrificial feelings and are at peace. When you get yourself to peace, you can break the cycle. This is a tremendously healing process. When you can genuinely get to a place where you can say, "I'm okay with that now," you will know that you are in control of your future decisions and that in the future you will do the right thing—for *you*.

CHAPTER 15

YOU KNOW HOW MUCH
I HATE YOU, RIGHT?

(Then you know how much I love you.)

As long as someone else is doing something to you, you don't have to look at your own stuff—and there is comfort in that.

I recently had a very bad day. It was like that Christmas movie where the ghost of the past keeps showing flashbacks of all the memories the character doesn't want to see.

Shortly after awakening I got a text from a lady whom I had never met or heard of before. She was dating someone I used to see, and she was in trouble. She recognized that she was being manipulated and didn't know how to get out of the situation or—frankly—if she was making it all up and getting in the way of her own happiness. I spent the better part of the day messaging with her and comforting her on multiple telephone calls.

I listened to her story with tears flowing down my face as I remembered my own hurt from this same man. And then there was a shift when ego stepped up. I was validated. I was right about this man's psychopathic behavior. I was right. I was right. I was right. It wasn't just me. It wasn't that I was hard to love. It wasn't that I was crazy. I was a victim who turned the tables on the predator, took action, and got away. I wanted to celebrate and gloat.

Of course, I couldn't say any of that out loud. I would have sounded shallow and bitter. As I went about my day and found myself sharing with my partner and family, I craved that one of them would say to me: "You were right about him. Thank goodness you can help warn other women and save them from the pain you kept going back to." But no one said anything other than that he needed to be held accountable. But what about me? What about my badge of honor for my superstar moves of getting away from him? What about: "You were right. You are so smart."

I started having dysfunctional relationships at a young age, and I carried a lot of guilt over having multiple romantic relationships in my past. And then I realized I was having the same failed relationship over and over. I remember the first disastrous relationship well. He had a great sense of humor, and we were well matched. I had created a fairy tale in my mind that we would someday be married, play beautiful music together and help people through our many talents within the church we both attended. He went off to bible college, and three months later he was engaged to someone else. That was one of the last times I went to church. What was the point? If good people could be so cruel, maybe I didn't want to strive to be one after all. Decades later, I was still dating emotionally unavailable men—men who cared far more about themselves than they did about me. I recognized how polluted my thinking had become because of the hurt, but even with that awareness I made excuses for people who treated me poorly. I grew accustomed to being alone in my relationships and managed to live relatively happy in that state.

A lot of my choices came from previous programming. From my family and my friends I have heard: "Maybe you should let us pick the next one" and "For someone so smart, you are sure stupid when it comes to men" and "You sure know how to pick them." On this no good very bad day, my need for validation, my need to shout from the rooftops that I was right, was just a side effect of the programming I had heard so often but had resisted believing.

Wounds from my past broke open, and the pain was fresh even though the relationships were all several years prior. I thought about my longest relationship and how dishonest he was with me and everyone else, including himself. The anger I felt about the wasted years was boiling just beneath the surface like a volcano that was ready to spew deadly lava over anything in its path. When it finally spilled over, it rolled down my cheeks as self-inflicted pain rather than flowing outward like I had imagined it would.

I opened up to a few friends and let the story unfold word after word, wound after wound. I needed release. It came unexpectedly and in a way that was vulnerable and open. Instead of being strong and powerful, I was fragile and gentle. The smallest obstacle would have stopped my release and shut me down. Instead, I perceived a comfortable silence in the room, and I kept talking. My words were my only way of letting go. There was no ego here, only humility, shame, and self-blame. I was not trying to heal my broken relationships. I was fixing myself, reprograming my thoughts and subsequent experiences.

I woke up the next day with no great freedom for having spoken my truth. Instead, I remembered my dream from the night before. It was a dream about not being heard. In my dream I was alone in a large gravel parking lot with no phone, no vehicle, no means of communicating, no one to listen. Just the dust left from a vehicle having driven away, the driver never looking back.

I needed to forgive myself for my choices. What mattered was that I recognized the behavior and begin to heal the pattern of the past so I was able to break free from the guilt and its hold over me. Simply said, as long as I felt bad about my stupid choices, I made more stupid choices and had more to feel bad about.

Recognizing patterns and choices is key in making better choices in the future. Although we do not have any control over what other people do, we can stop choosing the same types of relationships repeatedly. A quote credited to Einstein declares: "The definition of insanity is doing the same thing over and over again but expecting different results." If you recognize yourself in that quote, it's time to do some soul searching of your own.

Like so many other wounded people, I know the healing will come. I believe that. The key is to keep open, keep communicating, keep letting the light in, and slowly release all that I have been holding back at a pace that I am comfortable with, with people who deserve to hear, and whom I can trust to support me. If you have a wounded heart, do that.

And then some:

1. Celebrate! If you are reading this, you made it through your heartbreak and are on a path to self-actualization and a more peaceful and satisfying life. You are through the worst of it!

2. Release the anger, frustration, rage, hurt, all of it. There are gentle ways to do this, like productive conversations with a counselor or someone you can trust to help you work through your feelings. Be careful here—the goal is to move through your feelings, not to get stuck in your story.

3. Use gentle exercise or breathing to keep grounded in the moment as you visualize letting go of the pent-up anger and hurt. Release your pain with

breathwork, or journal your feelings. Studies have shown that suppressing anger often leads to depression; letting it go is not just desirable, but crucial.

4. If numbers 2 and 3 made you roll your eyes and gag a little, try this: join a martial arts or boxing class. This really works! Don't worry about being spiritual and loving, and instead visualize the person who hurt you and release. Don't hold back; let it all out. Run—as in literally—if it is safe for you to do so. If not, walk with purpose, pump your arms and fists and physically release the tension.

5. Take some time to contemplate or journal, asking yourself what you are drawing into your life through your thoughts. Notice without judgment any self-criticism that appears, and replace it with loving thoughts.

6. Forgive yourself. This takes time and practice. Do it daily. Visit www.victoriajohnson.org for more resources. Know that you were doing the best that you could do at the time.

7. Treat yourself as you would treat a good friend. Be gentle and loving and reassure yourself. Affirm that you can trust yourself and that you are loving and lovable.

8. Find the good in your life experience and reframe it in a way that you can be honestly grateful for. This does not mean just giving lip service about gratitude.

Start slowly with the will to heal your heart and move into a more loving and grateful space from there. When you can get to the place where you can reframe past hurts into something you can learn from while being thankful for the lesson, you can know that you are healed and unlikely to repeat the patterns of your past. It will happen; I am proof. You deserve to have that healing in your life. Allow life to lead you to what you desire.

CHAPTER 16

HAS YOUR GARDEN BEEN TAKEN OVER BY WEEDS?

(Grab them by the root and yank them out of your life.)

My dad could grow anything. His yard was always full of beautiful flowers, and he cultivated a plentiful garden. Even when he didn't have much room in his yard, he would find a little spot to plant cucumbers or tomatoes, or sneak in another rose bush. He always said it was to make my mother happy, but I suspect he just enjoyed the process of planting, growing and harvesting far more than she enjoyed the roses that bloomed. Our yard had several fruit trees and he would gather the fruit and preserve it in many different ways, all of which completely destroyed the kitchen! He was all in and completely dedicated to this process every year. While his friends would take summer holidays or spend weekends away visiting, he would stay home and diligently water and care for his bountiful garden and trees.

My father always gardened with love. He would look forward to the twice a day watering, the seemingly endless hours of picking berries, the pruning and even the weeding. It was all just part of what needed to be done in order to have a healthy garden.

Our relationships are like a garden. Some of us have a green thumb and maintain a healthy garden with ease and joy. Others are uncomfortable or harbor a grudge at having to maintain the garden and do as little as possible with it. They do just enough for it to be respectable and keep the neighbors happy! Those people spend more time complaining about it than they do nurturing it and resent the amount of time and commitment it seems to rob from them. Then there are those who fall right in the middle, and get by with what they have, only giving attention to what really needs their focus, overlooking the weeds until they become unmanageable. They are emotionally unattached, only seeing the garden as part of their existence, neither good or bad.

I have clients that seem to navigate through life much like the gardener who easily maintains a healthy garden. They are positive and seem to mostly attract positive people and experiences in their life. When a weed or toxic issue appears, they deal with it quickly and continue to nurture all that they have so lovingly created. This toxicity can show up as thoughts, people or circumstances, but its significance is kept to a minimum and the healthy garden is easily maintained.

Then there are the people who shift their focus off of what they are intending to grow and onto the weeds. I have coached and counseled Olivia on and off for many years. She has consented to the sharing of her story. It is not just her story—it is the story of so many people. Growing up, she felt she was often compared to other people. In her memory, no matter what she did, it was not enough. She firmly believes that other people are given an advantage and that she has to fight for everything that she has. She is convinced she has to work harder than others, just to maintain the status quo. When a competitive situation appears, she often becomes paralyzed by fear. She goes deep inside herself, gathers her strength and presents herself to the world as if success comes easy for her. What people don't see is that she is still terrified. She can't be happy about other people's success because she is too afraid of her own failure. She feels isolated and truly believes that it is her against the world. She would be the kind of gardener that yanks out the weeds by the root and then buries them under the dirt so that they are out of sight, but just under the surface they are once again taking root and getting ready to reappear.

It has been said that the quality of our life is determined by the quality of our thinking. It sounds simple, right? Just change our thinking. That is like telling someone to quit smoking because it is bad for their health. People already know that! They are stuck in habit, even when they don't want to be there. Instead of trying to break a habit, strive to dissolve it so that you are released of its hold on your life. To do this, first seek love and support from yourself. You can reach out to others once you have mastered the self-care and self-preservation that comes with truly loving yourself.

Going back to Olivia, she often can't even fathom a life where she is an equal, and certainly not one where the Universe is working for her rather than against her. When she is doing her personal growth work, she can begin to see the unhelpful coping strategies she is using and how to avoid them. Remember she buries the weeds so that they are out of sight. Olivia knows that she cannot thrive from a place of fear and strives to be connected to a higher power of her own understanding so that she can feel comfortable enough to move forward. Being that life is a process, sometimes she does this gracefully and other times with the force of a steamroller levelling anything or anyone who crosses her path. In those moments we minimize her fears by discussing them aloud. Often just a counseling conversation takes away some of the power that the fear holds over her. Together, we set up reminders to cue her to relax and breathe into her own healing. This helps her to return to the present moment and to a state of love. Just like the nasty weeds that try to take the energy and choke out the beautiful garden, fear tries to push the love out of Olivia's life and maintain control of her actions.

The third type of client is the gardener who is emotionally unattached to the outcome. Sometimes their life seems a little messy, and sometimes quite the opposite, and either way they are okay with it! They don't get sucked into the pressure, responsibility, or drama, they just do what needs doing on their own timeline and without guilt or negative emotions subtly manipulating them into action.

This client is the one who truly lives by the book title *What You Think of Me is None of My Business*, authored by Terry Cole-Whittaker. They practice self-care and know that they are masterpieces, and they do not seek perfection nor focus on the negative.

You might be thinking that it's easy for me to tell you to yank the toxic weeds out of your garden, but in your reality the toxicity is coming from relationships within your family. This can be tricky, and you may need a degree in horticulture to get through it, but you can do it! Let's start by looking at some different ways to manage the weeds that you can't just yank-out.

An important step is to get really clear on what is happening in the present moment. Is this person truly toxic or are you holding on to memories from the past? Do your best to repair the situation while accepting that sometimes your best will not be enough. Sometimes people twist words, don't listen and are not accountable for the damage they cause. Distancing yourself from those people will ensure a more plentiful garden. From time to time you have to remove the old to make way for the new. Healthy relationships improve all areas of your life while manipulative ones negatively impact you in all areas.

Examine what role you are playing in the stressful relationship, and try to determine what role you take when you are under stress. Are you a placater, blamer, super-reasonable or irrelevant person? World-renowned therapist Virginia Satir created these personality coping stances. What is your familiar go-to response, and what is the response when you are not under stress? Would your response change the other person's behavior? You may find that the answer is sometimes yes, sometimes no. What is important is that you learn to set healthy boundaries and then honor them.

Some examples of healthy boundaries could be agreeing to meet for breakfast or lunch and not dinner if you find the behavior escalates when alcohol is involved. Watch for patterns and then find ways to avoid volatile situations, such as holiday gatherings, by deciding when and where you will be, and having an exit strategy. If you put your boundaries in place and find that the toxicity continues to negatively impact your life, you may have to make the decision to cut ties either temporarily or permanently. Be confident in your proactive act of self-care. Remember this is your garden. Do that.

And then some:

1. Create what an experience is going to be like through affirmations and visualization.

2. In your mind, co-create a beautiful experience instead of something you are afraid of. As you

practice belief in these thoughts, they will become your reality.

3. Louise Hay taught that every word we speak and every thought we think is an affirmation. Start with your first thought of the day and create a loving and supportive experience through your thoughts. You can choose to feel good by choosing good thoughts and by becoming aware of what you draw into your life with your thoughts.

4. Examine your beliefs by running through your thoughts on a typical day. Examine what shows up for you and where you can choose a thought that serves you better. This can be done for all parts of your life, personally and professionally.

5. When you find yourself planting negative seeds, stop them from growing by asking yourself what you can do in the present moment to choose a more positive place to grow from. Give yourself a minute or two to listen for the answer. Stay in the now by asking yourself, *What can I do right now in this moment?*

6. With pen and paper make a list of the people in your life that you have a substantial relationship with. Divide a separate sheet of paper into left and right. On the left side, add the heading "Demote" and on the right side, add the heading "Promote." Swiftly place each relationship under either the left or right. You can always go back and re-examine your answers, but for this initial list, trust your instinct on where to place people.

7. Visualize each person, find ways to spend more or less time in the relationship in accordance with how they landed on your demote/promote list.

8. Remember that gardening is ongoing. Each day, week, month and season brings new development, new beauty and always changing conditions. Nothing is permanent, and you are the keeper of your garden.

CHAPTER 17

WE ARE HARD-WIRED FOR CONNECTION

(And I am not talking about the internet.)

It seems that so many men and women are searching for an elusive perfect mate. During the search they beat themselves up by comparing their traits to those of others and conjuring up ideas regarding the flawless relationships of their friends. They consider themselves a failure if their romantic relationship is headed down a road to nowhere, and then do what they can to get back on track, even when they know that the relationship is doomed to fail. I was an expert at this.

I tanked so many relationships that I wanted to give up and just enjoy the company of my cat, but something inside told me to keep trying. This is how I know that we are hardwired for connection. For me, it felt like my soul had always known that there was a different way than the way I had been living and wanted me to push forward until I found the mate my soul recognized and was connected to.

Along the way, there have been partners that I have loved, and partners that I have thought I loved, and partners that I really wanted to love me. There is a quote by Maya Angelou: "When someone shows you who they really are, believe them the first time."

I once had a relationship with a person who showed me so many different sides of himself that I was continuously off balance. He was a loving and kind person, who lied to me habitually, used jealousy and control as weapons, and then alternatively showed me love and treated me respectfully. He often celebrated my accomplishments publicly and then privately reminded me, "You are not as good as you think you are." He nurtured and loved me while ever so cleverly undermining my self-confidence. I had no idea how to take Maya's advice and figure out who it was that he was showing me and which part of him to believe.

In the year following that breakup, hardly a day went by that I didn't miss his companionship. The soft kisses, the words of affirmation, the holding hands everywhere we went. I didn't miss the dishonesty and the unwillingness to communicate. I was hurt and confused by how easily I was replaced by the next "most beautiful woman in the world."

One thing I know is this. When you love, you learn. I was able to recover from this relationship by spending time with people who truly loved and understood that I was in pain, no matter how illogical it seemed to be. Those people with whom I have a soul connection and who truly care about me. Not how I impact their life, but me, in all of my ugly truth at that moment.

One night, I sat outside with my friend in a state of complete brokenness. We hadn't seen each other in months, and I was listening to her tell me about her new romance. When I had a private moment, tears would trace their path down my face, but my smile would be there for her when she could see me. I wasn't jealous of what she was feeling, I was mourning the loss of what I thought I had.

She could see through me. She could see my pain. She quickly snapped a picture of me with her cell phone and turned it around to show me. She asked me what I saw. I saw only pain, heaviness and darkness. Why was I still crying every day? I was the one who ended it, and for good reason, so why was I wanting to call him, and to reach out to him every day? No matter how many pep talks I gave myself, in my private moments the pain was still at the surface.

Having a true soul friend to speak with, I was able to remember the reasons why the relationship was toxic, and to forget about how he made me feel more loved than I had ever felt before. The relationship had awoken a piece inside of me that I had put to sleep a long time ago. That little girl that wanted to be nurtured and loved, just for who she was. She was the one who was devastated. The adult me has always been so strong, because I felt that I had to be. Once I opened up and succumbed to feel this kind of pain, it was overwhelming to me and I didn't know what to do with it. I was continuously fighting the urge to turn on the TV, scroll through Facebook, or go to the refrigerator—anything to shut off the pain instead of feeling it.

There was a part of me that knew that I was at a crossroads. I could choose to continue numbing my feelings, or face head-on the reality that my mind houses a lost and lonely little girl who just wants to be loved unconditionally for who she is. It is also home to a woman who knows that she deserves real love. I knew that this pattern of choosing the wrong relationships had to end.

I knew that to connect with the right people, I had to heal from within, starting with *feeling* the pain and loss and moving through it. This time the answer would not be found in putting on an outfit that makes me feel good, doing my hair, having a manicure or accomplishing something that I would receive acknowledgement for, but really feeling the pain. It was awful, but I somehow knew that from that place of complete surrender and total loss of control, I could find my way back to myself. Maybe for the first time in decades.

Being in the wrong relationship, or worse, a relationship where there is emotional manipulation is like one of those spectacular but delicate 3D puzzles. It stands together nicely, balanced because the right piece has found its way into the pieces that support it. Emotional manipulation begins to pull out pieces here and there. It starts in places that you can't see, but makes you feel like something is just not right. The puzzle shifts and adjusts its weight, quite naturally, but still feels a little bit off. Eventually enough pieces are taken away that it crumbles; it is unrecognizable.

This is when the manipulative relationships around us have taken control. They place pieces back together by forcing them together where there is no natural fit. They create their own masterpiece—something in the manipulator's image, something that reflects how they see the world. There may be gaping holes, leaning foundations, or puzzle pieces left over to discard or to reserve for later use. It is not in harmony with the essence of what the puzzle once was, but it is still standing, and if you don't look too closely from the outside, you don't see the damage or how fragile it is.

If you have the help of someone accurately reflecting the situation back to you, sharing words of affirmation, truth, and encouragement, you begin to remember your previous magnificence. Using the puzzle analogy, you can try to hide the holes where the pieces don't quite fit, but until there is a complete dismantling, the puzzle will not stand strong.

When you start again and rebuild from the beginning, you have the opportunity to lay a strong foundation, to use your own values for pillars, and to construct the walls with harmony and stability. Some pieces of your life will come together quickly, some will take time and have to be tried from a few different angles. If you persevere, in the end you'll have a creation that is strong from the inside out. Your inner self becomes both a fortress and a place to love. It becomes an inner self that only you can dismantle, for you have learned that your power comes from knowing and trusting yourself, and you no longer allow or tolerate someone else to shape your destiny. You recognize sabotaging behavior and when someone shows you who they are, you believe them the first time!

Your friendships and work relationships also play a big part in how connected you feel. The people around us often mirror back our behavior. When we grow our social connections in a positive way, we have a positive result. A socially-empowered person achieves more peace and fulfillment basically because of their ability to be connected. People around them want to help catapult them to success. They earn the trust and all-out support of people, and achieve their goals while helping, lifting up, and supporting other people. They maximize their social potential as naturally as taking their next breath.

For others, it doesn't come quite so naturally. Whether it's a romantic relationship, or one with family, friends or co-workers, learning to cultivate genuine connections begins with a willingness to put yourself out there and keep trying. I have taken many courses over the last three decades on building relationships and human connection. Through them, I have learned more about myself, and therefore more about effective communication, and most importantly, that not everything is about me! Do that.

And then some:

1. Be genuine. Show a genuine interest in other people.
2. Be the greatest listener that you can be. Ask questions and listen to the answers. I am embarrassed to admit that I spent years and years pretending to listen while formulating my response in my mind instead. Just listen; it is about the other person and not about you. Do not just hear them out, listen to them with your heart. Make eye contact when the person talks to you. Listen as if every word matters, because it does. This is something I still work on every day, so please be kind and patient with yourself, and know that creating new habits takes time.

3. Laugh out loud. Find your funny bone and don't take yourself too seriously all the time. It can be movies, kids, animals, even hilarious YouTube videos. The moment you allow yourself to laugh, you raise your vibrational energy. Laughter releases natural feel-good endorphins and makes your interactions with others memorable long after the event has passed.

4. Don't forget yourself. Even though we are talking about forming meaningful connections, know that

you are the most important part of that interaction. Value yourself before anyone else. If you deem yourself respectable and worthy of affection, people will be drawn to you. This is not selfish; it is self-care.

5. Perform random acts of kindness. I know this is not a new concept, but it is still powerful and relevant. Little acts of kindness can be as simple as giving someone a card, text or email, or holding a door open for someone. As children most of us we were taught to be good citizens, showing kindness and thoughtfulness. Revive the good deeds and this time let them stay for good!

6. Contact some old friends. Some past friendships are better left dormant. Thanks to technology, you can re-live the good old days by scrolling through social media to look for the people with whom you want to communicate with again.

7. Develop your personality. Learn your preferred communication styles and why others communicate the way they do. Visit www.personalitydimensions.com for more information on Personality Dimensions®.

8. Developing self-awareness cultivates confidence. Confidence attracts connection; arrogance breaks it. Enough said.

9. Keep nurturing your relationships. Your relationship with your family, friends and significant others are precious and part of who you are. (Often family

relationships teach us the most about ourselves.) As you learn to manage your emotions, you will find yourself surrounded by others who have the same commitment to personal development as you do.

10. Above all, trust your instincts. If a relationship is not meant for you, let it go. Remember Maya Angelou's wise words of advice. Believe them the first time.

SECTION FOUR

YOUR PROSPERITY: BREAK DOWN BARRIERS AND CHOOSE AN ABUNDANT LIFE

CHAPTER 18

YOU CAN'T HIT A TARGET YOU CAN'T SEE

(Take off the blinders of self-doubt and fear to uncover your vision for the future.)

We all look at life through different lenses. It is part of what makes us who we are. It doesn't matter where you are in life right now, how many mistakes you've made, opportunities you've passed up, or what's happened to you in life, you can get clear on your goals and start moving in the direction of your desires. This chapter addresses overcoming self-doubt, knowing where you are headed, and how to believe in yourself enough to get there. It is within your power, and it will change your life completely.

Self-doubt has a ripple effect that spreads into many different areas of life. For most of us, self-doubt has impacted our past, is influencing our decisions in the present moment and will continue unless we reveal and heal our self-doubt and identify what is holding us back.

When I look back on my life, I can see how many times I was held back from setting a goal—never mind reaching it—because of self-doubt. I hear this regularly from my coaching clients as well. Doubt allows fear to get in the way of doing anything. This can turn into a severe lack of motivation to do more than you have to just to get by. We may want to do more, but fear causes us to procrastinate.

When we are not clear on our goals and are full of doubt and fear, we miss opportunities, experience regret and eventually accept that we are a failure, or incapable of seeing things through.

Not believing in ourselves often stems back to negative messages we began to believe about ourselves in our learning years.

I knew at a young age that I had the inner strength to take on tasks beyond my years. That meant that I started many things—and left many things unfinished. I had big goals and dreams, and then would get distracted by the next shiny thing that caught my attention. Over time, this lessened because I could always hear my mother's voice saying that I never finish anything I start. Eventually things that I was on track with, I would sabotage and not finish. And then I moved on to not starting things at all because I didn't want to go through the negative self-talk that made me feel guilty, shameful, or incapable if I didn't finish them.

This became an ongoing story in my life. Even when I would make a healthy choice by changing a behavior, I could hear that voice saying that I never finish anything I start. In my early forties I decided to silence this voice once and for all. I started to train for an ultramarathon even though I had never even completed a marathon before. I trained with the sole focus of finishing what I started. I visualized obstacles and ways to manage my thoughts and performance if the obstacle appeared. I focused on one kilometer at a time. I practiced with the course outline taped to my treadmill, and on event day I was ready to go. I learned some valuable life lessons in the 8 hours and 29 minutes it took me to complete the ultramarathon. I learned that when I turned to look behind me, it slowed me down and took me a few steps to get back on track, and I learned that consistently taking forward action got me where I was going. I learned to focus on me, not on the other participants. I finished four hours faster than I expected and as I crossed that finish line, I promised myself that the negative message that was haunting me would never have power over me again.

Within minutes of finishing, I called my mother from my cell phone. She was surprised that I was finished already and exclaimed "You're done already? When you decide to do something, you do it." That is the message I have decided to listen to from now on.

Knowing how we developed self-doubt helps us recover. We can work toward building belief in ourselves so that we can reduce or overcome self-doubt. Many people learn to put off their dreams and limit their ideas due to well-meaning parents who are also stuck in their own self-doubting lives and cannot ever envision anything different. Parents don't want to keep their kids from dreaming. But when their child tells them about their big dream to travel the world or become a writer and so on, parents react in fear and make statements that may be statistically true but that limit the child and squash their confidence.

For example, they might discourage their child from becoming a writer by telling them no one makes money writing, or they might discourage their child from becoming anything that is above what they themselves are capable of due to the fear of the child being hurt or disappointed. This is only due to their own limited thinking that was likely passed on to them by well-meaning parents as well. My intent is not to blame parents or make them wrong—parents do the best they can with the information and skills they have at the time. This way of thinking becomes the way of thinking for most children as they grow into adulthood. Statistically most people do not break out of the financial class they were born into. The exciting thing to remember, though, is that there are people who are able to envision possibilities and then take action to see them through regardless of limited beliefs and negative messaging. They have learned to release self-doubt, or not even embrace it to begin with, set goals, dream big, and achieve what others may never even have considered.

You were born with everything you need to experience

success in life. Your success may look different from someone else's and that's okay. You really do deserve to have a happy, fulfilled life that you enjoy. Consider all that you have successfully done in the past, and focus your attention there to grow your confidence. You have read it before in this book, and you will likely read it again—you are not alone. You are enough. You are deserving, and you are perfectly you.

Train your mind to overcome limiting beliefs, fears and doubts by transforming them into positive affirmations. Change the focus from the thought of what you can't do to what is possible. Remember my story of overcoming my self-doubt with a 56-kilometer walk/run? I didn't focus on not finishing. Instead, I kept my mind, body, and enthusiasm aimed at the same target, the finish line.

An effective way to build confidence and clarify your goals is to create a vision board for yourself. You know how companies have vision statements? Well, you are the CEO of you. Have a vision, and document it. Make a plan, write it down. Knowing that the Universe often just laughs at our detailed plans, keep your focus on the end result.

I have been practicing this technique for many years. Louise Hay, author of *You Can Heal Your life*, founder of Heal Your Life Workshops and Hay House and one of my teachers and mentors, was teaching this long before it became mainstream by Law of Attraction,

Oprah, and the release of the book and movie, *The Secret.*

Get into a good creative headspace before you begin. Instead of thinking of everything you want and do not have, think about all of the things you have created. Do you have a roof over your head? Awesome. You did that! Do you have relationships that make you happy? Awesome, you did that, too. Mentally prepare by thinking about some key areas in your life: relationships, health, wellness, spirituality, career or financial prosperity. Think big—the sky is the limit—super-duper dream! Remember to ask that adorable sweet innocent little child in you what it is that they want to see come true.

I have found there is no one right way to do this. There is just your way. Let your personality shine not only on your goals for the vision board, but also in how you choose to create it. Do you need to spend a day thinking about this, a week, or is more than five minutes too long? All of those strategies are right—just choose the one that is best for you.

I'm an action person. That means I do a lot of things more than once. What I mean is, I do it, then I decide I don't want it that way and I do it again. And you know what? That is okay. It is actually impossible to do your vision board wrong. So seriously, exhale, and get to it.

You may be pumped and thinking, yes, let's do it! Let the co-creating begin! Or you might be wondering exactly why you would ever, ever want to do this. It is not all

141

about being new age, spiritual or mindful. It is about you. It is about you getting clear on what you want and then following those dreams. It is for those times when your confidence is wavering, and self-doubt is creeping in. Your vision board will keep you focused and serve as a daily reminder that your goals and dreams matter and are achievable.

Whether you are a lone wolf, a vision board partier, or a parent looking for something to do with your kids, the method isn't important. What is important is that you set aside the time to do this. I have found that once you are in the process, you are able to stay there. For my last vision board creation, I set aside three hours and was able to really get into the process—which I admit, shocked me because I have a short attention span! I was in a creative environment where I felt supported and created my very own visual masterpiece.

To create a vision board, gather photos, words and symbols to represent several areas of your life. You may wish to design your board using the topics of this book— health, relationships, passion and spirituality. Make sure your words, pictures and symbols speak to your heart and not just what you think your vision *should* be. Write statements as if you are already living them—use *I am* or *I have,* instead of *I want* or *I need.* You can google vision boards for other practical how-to ideas.

When you have completed your vision board, put it in a place where you can see it and admire it daily. I sometimes keep mine in the kitchen, so that I am connected with it regularly, and I sometimes put it in the bedroom where it is the first thing I see in the morning. I lay in bed half asleep and do a quick review of what I am creating. Another great idea is to take a photo of it and put it on your cell phone as your lock screen so that you are seeing it several times a day without setting aside time to focus on it! Resist the urge to be impatient or compare where you where you are at in the present moment to where you think you should be. Trust in the process.

There are many ways that vision boards can work for you. Just the act of creating the vision board raises your energy to match the energy you would have if you already had the things on the board! It increases confidence. It helps you to see that you can have the life of your dreams and pushes away fear. If you follow the Law of Attraction, defined as "that which is like unto itself is drawn," you create a space where you believe you can have what you desire. The more high-vibrating affirmative energy you put toward it, the more your vision becomes your reality! Do that.

And then some:

1. Use your board to remind you of your goals on a daily basis.

2. Congratulate yourself for the small steps. Maybe you haven't mastered the downward dog pose; but if you walked around the block or made good food

choices, you are due for a high vibration celebration.

3. Put some thought into these questions: What would my life look like if I had everything just how I want it? What would be the best part of that? Then, really connect with that feeling. Just like an athlete visualizes their event, visualize your life in the way you want it to be. See it, feel it, and get ready to live it.

4. Examine where the limiting beliefs are showing up in your life. Make a plan to overcome them by finding new people to surround yourself with and replace old habits with new activities. Letting go of the things that no longer serve you creates room in your life for the things that do.

5. Talk to someone who understands how you're trying to change your life and get over self-doubt. This may be a professional, a life coach, a friend or someone from a support group. The important thing is to cultivate positive support people as part of your team.

6. Stop thinking about the doubt and fear. It's better to try to shelve the negative thoughts and really live in the moment. Being in the present enables you to truly realize that life is full of unlimited possibility.

7. Set small, immediate goals to encourage you. Success can be as small as getting up in the morning, to going out to an event, to creating something to gift to yourself or someone else. When obstacles arise,

instead of letting them push you into self-doubt, respect that they are just another tool that helps you reach your goals.

8. Celebrate you. In big ways, in small ways, just always remember to celebrate who you are and all that you have accomplished thus far in life. You are amazing.

CHAPTER 19

GET OFF THE FENCE
BETWEEN FEAR AND FAITH

*(And cheers to other f-words that
will show up in the process.)*

We all have difficult situations and deal with difficult people from time to time. Occasionally, we are that difficult person. For me, there have been periods in my life where I became paralyzed by a situation and incapable of making a decision and moving forward. This chapter and the following three chapters are to help you move through those feelings and into a passionate and financially rewarding life.

Within the day to day of meeting deadlines, fulfilling obligations, and trying to enjoy your life, it can be hard to find time to tackle difficult emotions and deal with them appropriately.

Difficult emotions are as much a part of life as positive feelings, and by learning to accept these emotions, express them productively, and handle them proactively, you can learn from your emotions and become a stronger, more balanced person.

It is key to learn to accept rather than avoid your difficult emotions. Learn to experience your negative feelings in ways that are beneficial to you long-term. Focus your energy on activities that are productive and healthy for processing your emotions, rather than pushing difficult feelings away.

My coaching client Trevor has agreed to share his story about being fired from a prestigious job and the emotional trauma that followed. Trevor had been working in upper management for several years when he decided to leave a job due to stress. After a few months, his health better, he decided to go back into corporate work. He was hired as executive director for a non-profit organization that he had no real interest in, but he felt that taking the job was the right thing to do. (For a reminder about self-sacrifice, refer back to Chapter 14.)

Everything went fairly smoothly for the first few months. The board of directors was made up of professional women, and he and his assistant were the only males at the monthly board meetings. He did not have an issue with reporting directly to an all-female board, but he did have an issue with them being stuck in the way things have always been and being unwilling to look at change for the future. Trevor was able to make some positive changes and received a great deal of support from the general membership and the people who benefited from the services of the non-profit. Even with these small wins, every day going into work became a struggle. Each day was the same. He would give himself a mental pep talk while shaving and preparing to go into work. *Today is going to be different*, he would tell himself. And it never was. Instead he was without clear direction as one board member would provide positive feedback on an issue while another would provide negative feedback on the same issue. He felt paralyzed and unable to fill up the hours in the day with activity because the organization was so stuck in doing things the old way. One morning the president of the board came into his office and fired him on the spot. She said they had decided to go a different direction. He was flabbergasted and could only conclude that they liked to talk about change but not really implement it and that he had just been pushing them too far. A piece of him felt relieved, and the rest of him felt scared, humiliated and ashamed.

He took ten minutes and packed up his personal items and then headed down to his parking spot. Once there he sat in his car for an hour and then drove around for an hour more trying to gather his thoughts and courage to go home and face his wife and two young girls. He felt genuinely scared that they were not going to be able to make it financially. They had just finished paying off the past due bills from his hiatus and now he was unemployed again. It was a few days before Christmas and everyone's mood was high and celebratory. How was he ever going to walk through that door and tell them that he had been fired?

He didn't. Instead he went home at the usual time and stayed with the usual routine. He "took some time off from work" because it was the holidays and wouldn't have to go through the motions of going back to work until the kids went back to school in the first week of January. When Trevor thought about what he was going to do on that early January day, he felt sick to his stomach. He blocked out those feelings by drinking too much—it was the holidays after all. He created stories in his mind about how closed minded that group of dinosaurs that called themselves a board were, and how they would be begging him to come back in no time. But the phone never rang, and Trevor had to prepare for the inevitable—telling his wife and children that he was unemployed—again.

Over the next few months Trevor suffered from anxiety and panic attacks. All the emotions he had suppressed were finding their way out one way or another. He had bouts of depression and cut himself off socially. He got to the point where he was unemployable the way he was, further adding to the anxiety.

A counselor recommended that Trevor start seeing a coach for strategies on how to get back into the workforce in a way that he was comfortable with. This is where I entered the picture. We did a lot of work around suppressed emotions and clarifying his goals for the future. He began to feel hopeful, and the more hopeful he became, the less stress and depression he experienced.

We worked together to help Trevor identify his difficult feelings. He learned to assess how well he was handling them when they arose, and to recognize when he was using avoidance as a coping strategy. He learned to be proactive, changing the way he approached difficult emotions from their start.

Those feelings that are often the most difficult for us to grapple with are also those that raise the most intense emotions. The most common difficult feelings that you may struggle with include loneliness, anger, sadness, and pain, but all of these essentially stem from the same emotion, which is fear. Whether we are afraid of being alone, afraid of losing something or someone, or afraid of emptiness in our lives, fear is a powerful emotion and guides our hearts and minds in many instances.

While you may choose to look at these emotions as negative or difficult, you could instead choose to accept that these feelings are a part of life. They provide us with opportunities to learn more about ourselves, they teach us how to handle problems more effectively, and they can help us develop empathy for others. Difficult emotions also teach us about the unresolved issues that may lay in our past or are a part of our present.

Listening to your difficult feelings and the emotions they trigger inside you can be an effective tool for recognizing when things are not working in your life. These emotions, while strong, can serve as a compass for pinpointing problems in your life that you could choose to address.

These strong feelings can help you identify paths to solutions, in many cases, or even help you create new boundaries in your life that will safeguard against future turmoil.

Listening to your difficult feelings, instead of ignoring them, is a healthy way to cope with them as well as learn the valuable lessons in life that help you grow. Becoming attuned to your strong emotions, checking in regularly, and even talking with yourself and others about your difficult feelings can become part of your path toward greater happiness and lifelong mental health. Your emotions give you valuable information about yourself and your life, and learning to hear these messages is an important skill to learn and cultivate. Instead of viewing your negative or strong emotions as enemies, embrace them as friends and helpful contributors to your life. When you embrace them, you can learn from them. Do That.

And then some:

1. Identify who and what ignites strong emotion for you. Often we are most emotional when someone reflects back a part of us that we don't want to look at.

2. When you see these reflections, you have the opportunity to make them a part of your growth. Just by being aware of your true feelings and emotions, you can make them a welcome part of

your life and therefore deal with them more effectively and respond appropriately when triggered and under fire.

3. Avoid buying into the belief that you should be happy all the time or that strong emotions are negative. Decide to embrace challenges like a friend you were expecting. I am not suggesting that you sit around waiting for the worst to happen, but rather that you have the faith that you can conquer any situation that presents itself by facing it head on, however uncomfortable it may feel in the moment.

4. Focus on your goals. Let go of any guilt associated with success. For free resources on this please visit www.victoriajohnson.org.

CHAPTER 20

MY SUBCONSCIOUS MADE ME DO IT

(… again, and again and again.)

Have you ever jumped in your car to go to the grocery store and instead ended up turning toward your workplace? Have you ever driven your vehicle and were so involved with a conversation with friends or engrossed in your thoughts that you just drove to your destination without noticing? Do you have a daily routine that you could do in your sleep? Well, in a way, you are. That is your subconscious at work.

Our subconscious mind is like the world's most capable computer and it is always updating without us even realizing it. Research shows that our conscious mind is responsible for about 15% of our thinking. Our subconscious mind takes over and puts us on auto-pilot for the other 85%. We want our subconscious mind to be a goal achieving, success mechanism. To learn more about how to obtain that, keep on reading.

We are often so busy trying to manage everything in front of us that we forget that the subconscious already has it all worked out. It stores our thoughts, experiences, information we have learned, and emotions that were implied as "memory."

The subconscious mind is useful in two ways. The first way involves receiving information, solving problems, and receiving inspiration. The second way deals with programming your mind to supercharge your confidence, your self-image, and your desired beliefs. This can take a little time at first but like many things gets easier with practice.

Awareness is the first step. Once you recognize that you need to make changes—then what? Visualization is a great tool for beginning to create the changes you desire. Programming your subconscious works best through visualization because pictures and symbols effectively impact your subconscious. With visualization, your mind processes information and absorbs it with the symbolic images.

Our subconscious mind never rests. Whatever goal or problem we present to the subconscious, it will work on continually. Whatever we think deeply with emotion makes a strong impression on our subconscious mind. This is a blessing and a curse, because our thoughts and worries can negatively impact what we are trying to create.

Often we hear people tell stories of their childhood and vow that they will raise their children differently. They examine the relationships that their parents had with each other and with others and decide that is not how they will be doing things. They joke about their parents' interests or hobbies and complain about how they do things. One day the joke is over because they realize that they have themselves become their father or mother. They are repeating the same rules to the children, communicating the same, engaging in the same interests, or managing their home and time within the same patterns that were modeled to them by their parents. Their subconscious made them do it.

The subconscious can be reprogrammed over time. Part of it is by being very careful what we think. When we truly believe that our every thought is creating our future, we become aware of the importance of each thought. Studies have shown that most of our thoughts throughout the day are similar and show up repeatedly. The Law of Attraction teaches that a belief is just a thought you keep thinking, and Louise Hay's proverb applies as well: "It's only a thought, and a thought can be changed."

When working toward a more proactive mindset, it is important to also watch the language you use to talk to yourself and others about your difficult emotions. Your words say a lot about what you believe to be possible, and changing how you talk about your feelings has the power to alter how you are actually feeling. Instead of focusing on "Why can't I ...?" (do or have something), reframe the conversation to instead be about "How can I ...?" (accomplish my goal). "I want to ..." could be the focus of your goal setting and work, rather than worrying over what you do or do not deserve to have.

When life gets hard, you may find you keep reverting back to old behaviors. Rather than focus on why you can't stop doing what you are doing, instead reframe your words to be about what you would like to be doing. Focus on how you can change the situation instead of just accepting that is how it is. Instead of making excuses for not having enough time or being too busy, focus on how you can make changes that will give you more time to do what is important to you.

Reactive people focus on why others cannot change, whereas proactive people accept others for who they are and instead focus on meeting their own needs.

When you decide to accept your difficult emotions and become more proactive in how you handle yourself when they arise, you realize that those strong feelings can teach you a great deal in life. Acceptance helps you to let go of patterns that are no longer serving you. It allows you to admit the truth of your situation as well as your own personal strengths and areas for growth. You have more energy to deal with your emotions in a healthy way, because you are not trying to avoid or push them away. Acceptance allows you to pursue your goals and make progress toward a healthier version of yourself. Do that.

And then some:

1. Acknowledge your emotions. It is completely okay to feel your feelings; you do not need to push them away.

2. As you become familiar with what triggers your emotions and how you react to yourself and others when experiencing difficulty, you will gain empathy toward others who also may be experiencing difficulty in their lives. Give yourself the same grace you would give others and get in touch and stay with the uncomfortable feelings.

3. Avoidance does not teach you new behaviors or help you set new goals. Learning to accept your emotions also means you see that they are often not as bad as you anticipated, and they will pass with time. It takes the fear out of the equation and teaches you that you are strong enough to change the patterns of your subconscious. Keep a section in a journal where you can write down in bullet form each pattern that you see in your life. Decide what you would like to change from that list.

4. Transform your beliefs regarding the pattern you want to change by choosing different thoughts and words. Use visualization to create a different outcome. Each night when you go to bed and each morning immediately upon waking, spend some time visualizing what it is you want to achieve that day and what you want your life to look like.

Visualization connects you with the feeling of having what you want, which is the most effective way to change.

5. Become aware of the language that you use so that you are expressing a positive outcome. For example, you could replace, "I can't wait to start my new job" with "I'm excited to start my new job."

6. In the words of world-renowned cell biologist Bruce Lipton: "Whatever I am perceiving out there I will manifest a physical complement to it in here. So if I have a healthy vision, my mind's chemistry converts my body into health. If I live in fear …. Fear causes 90% of the illness on the planet. And it's all generated by the perceptions of the mind." The picture you hold in your mind creates the behavior and biology you express in life. You are not a victim of anything other than the programs you are operating from. Change the programs you are operating from. If your subconscious programs match the wishes and desires of the conscious mind, your life will be one continuous honeymoon experience for as long as you live on this planet. To change the programs, repetition is key. Keep repeating the thoughts that you want to be your reality.

7. For more information on the subconscious mind, visit www.brucelipton.com. Often.

CHAPTER 21

WHAT HAPPENS WHEN YOU GET A TASTE OF SUCCESS?

(It's like Chinese food. You are satisfied in the moment, but an hour later you want more.)

I have known a book was ready to explode out of me since I was in my early teens, maybe even younger. I was drawn to pen and paper like the proverbial moth to a flame. I found the urge to write irresistible. It gave me a place to release my innermost secrets, fears and, because I was a teenager, love and subsequent heartbreak (and repeat). I also knew the danger. If I spoke my truth out loud, it would be challenging for me and would negatively impact other people. Yet the bright light of that flame kept calling me. At times I would come so close that I could feel the heat of the flame on the thin veil of aloofness I was hiding behind. Somehow, the danger was too much, the vulnerability too real, and so I kept my words safely stored away in the dark corners of my mind and heart (and journal).

In my twenties, I skirted around being a serious writer. I confined myself to journaling and journaling and journaling. There were hundreds of tear-stained pages. They outlined each painful experience invariably painting myself protagonist and everyone else as the villain. I was both crucified and mourned depending on the mood and the day and whether or not wine was involved. If I had published a book then, I am sure an appropriate title could have been, *Don't Do This & Definitely Don't Do That!* Looking back over the pages to remember how horribly I had been wronged would instantly produce another bucket of tears, anger, and poor-me-ity.

After the tears had dried, I had enough filled-up journals to create a large and long bonfire. Literally. It was a magical night in my thirties. I had friends over and we all committed to letting go of the pain of our past. Burning the pages was wonderful and symbolic. But until the memories burned in my mind were healed, it was an empty gesture. Speaking for myself, I was stuck in my story.

In my thirties, I wrote magazine and newspaper articles and left my journaling for more sporadic events and self-reflection urges. I was trying to figure out who I was, and I was fighting for survival with two teenage boys and a business to build from the ground up. Still I longed to write.

In my forties, I continued to write articles, and I added a trilogy of children's books to my resume. It was exhilarating to see that wish come true and I wanted more. It left me hungry for the books that I knew were mine for the writing, in particular, this book.

In my fifties, I was committed to getting this sucker out. I had been pregnant with it for almost forty years. Moses and the Israelites wandered in the desert for forty years, but that seemed to be the turning point. It was for me as well. I took on many speaking engagements and found my love for sharing this work. Each time I would get in front of a group of people and share the principles and experiences from this book, I would have an adrenaline rush that could only be satisfied by doing it again. There is something about having people relate to my experience and solutions and then finding hope for their own healing that is deeply satisfying. And I continue to be hungry for doing more.

Doing more does not have to mean writing a book. It means to do more of what leaves you feeling satisfied, full to the top, and yet longing for more. Celebrate all that you have accomplished so far and pay close attention to what it is that ignites a spark within you. Do more of that!

Recently my granddaughter was reviewing my vision board for this year. She was reading the captions from the bottom of the board to the top to show off her amazing reading skills. I have "experience the magic" on the board to remind me that there are things that just work out without my intervention, and it is okay to experience it as magic rather than being afraid of it. Above that I have the phrase "stories of success." I was half listening to her and half reading through some articles I had written in my thirties when she looked at me and said, "Experience the magic of success."

An awareness hit me that I had completely missed. All of these feelings of not accomplishing my desire and somehow having failed by not getting my writing out there were all an illusion I had created in my mind, because in my hand I was holding twenty-year-old published writing of mine. I had minimized my writing because I had been so busy counting my shortcomings as a writer that I forgot to celebrate that I have been a published writer for several years already. I had been building my skills and working on my dream all along. That doesn't mean that I have loved every experience. I often read back and squirm a little but for the most part I am impressed with the young writer within me who was brave enough to taste what she wanted to pursue.

So often we forget to experience the magic of the journey. We have bumps along the road that set us back in our career and instead of realizing that they are part of the magic of our success we consider them failures. Sometimes, we not only let them slow us down; we let them stop us.

Consider this, if you had everything just how you want it in your career aspirations, what would that look like for you? What would it do for you? The chances are very good that you already have part of that epic win working in your life right now. If you want to be a top-ranking CEO earning buckets of money and are currently a middle manager earning reasonable income, you are well on your way! You are not a failure for what you don't have, but rather a success for everything you have done so far! Your burning desire is showing up in your expression right now in this moment. You are creating your future. Experience the magic of your success! Be satisfied with what you have and hungry for more of what your heart desires. Do that.

And then some:

1. Think about your burning desire for your career. Think about the big picture. Span decades if appropriate. Document it, and take it all in.

2. What have you considered an epic fail in the past in this area? For example, were you fired, did you take time off for other things, did you lose sight of your burning desire?

3. Reframe your epic fail. What was the result of it? What did you learn from it? How did it bring you closer to your burning desire? What turned out to be a blessing or a benefit?

4. Spend some time thinking about what the best part of achieving your burning desire is. From this, identify your core value around this.

5. Find the areas in your life where this core value is already showing up, and celebrate that win daily to stay in alignment with what you truly desire.

6. What gives you an adrenaline rush when you think about doing it? Is this a passion that you can pursue?

CHAPTER 22

PLEASE UNIVERSE, DON'T LEAVE ME NOW

(For times when you find yourself running toward the mama bear when everyone says you should lie down and play dead.)

You know those moments when you are so scared by the leaps of faith that you are taking that you literally can't sleep at night? Some people call it worry; others reframe it as excitement. For me it is usually fear showing up.

I recently hired someone to manage both me (good luck with that!) and my digital platform—YouTube videos, websites, and so on. The goal is that he manages strategy moving forward so that I can focus on the creative stuff and helping people to move forward and transform their lives. I long to be connected with people on a heart level and know that is not going to happen when I am buried in a pile of paper at my desk and an even bigger 'things to do' pile. I long to connect with people so that I can touch that place deep inside of them and they will know that they are not alone. I want to help people find hope. That isn't going to happen if I keep myself chained to my desk.

Hiring someone and paying them to do something I had been doing myself for years was terrifying. What if I had a slow month? Where was this money going to come from? I knew that I had to quit playing small and take myself seriously. I had to run straight toward what I considered to be dangerous territory. I wanted to run back to safety, but safety wasn't helping me live my dream. It reminded me of the warnings I have heard about bear encounters—back away slowly, don't look them in the eye, play dead if you need to. Instead I was looking that bear in the face and running full speed toward her. It seemed a little crazy (even to me), but I knew that I could either *hope* to live out my passion or *commit* to making it happen.

For the first few months every time I sent that monthly salary, I felt sick to my stomach. I thought about that amount of money (which was huge to me) that was transferring out of my account every month instead of into it. More fear. More ego reasoning. Well, you know, I could probably do what he does and keep the money. Then the spiritual side would chime in with: "Victoria, I thought you wanted to focus on helping people, not on all of the little details of the behind-the-scenes stuff." The little girl would answer with: "I do, but I am scared. Scared of spending money that I have worked so hard for, scared of surrendering control to someone else, scared of not controlling the outcome, scared of putting my faith in someone else." Then my Divine being would

166

chime in with soothing words like: "It's okay, you are on the right path, stay true to your passion, everything is going to be alright, keep moving forward."

In those moments the voice I wanted to listen to most was the voice of ego. The one that reassured me that I could do it all myself and didn't need to depend on anyone else. The problem was that I had been listening to that voice for decades, and it always repeated the same pattern. I would do well, really well, and then I would plateau, and then I would burn out. I didn't want that this time. I wanted to stay true to my passion to help others learn to love themselves more and subsequently grow and teach others to love themselves more.

There's no such thing as overnight success. Most people who appear to have overnight success have been working on it for years. Keep moving toward your dreams and they will show up in your life. Consider the things that you already have, realizing that those are things you once wished for.

Be ready to make some mistakes and when you do, know that it is part of the process. Don't quit. There is a saying: "When the student is ready, the teacher will appear." We are all here to learn our lessons. Our parents, school teachers, friends, colleagues, officemates, neighbors— they are our teachers. When we run toward our fears, we find the road to our personal dreams. Just ask any successful person—chances are they had to get a little uncomfortable to get where they are now!

When I think of the ripple effect that staying true to my passion could bring, it brings tears to my eyes. The fear-based nausea subsides, and I can gladly send payment to my team and all of the resources that support me. The lesson here is to be brave in the face of fear. Break the cycle. Take that leap of faith. Trust yourself. Know that you are worth investing in. As it turns out, I have recovered many times over the money that I have paid out. I have also felt supported and have embraced many new ideas. The only way for me to move to the next level of my career was to let someone help me. My life has been enriched far beyond dollars and cents. My passion and purpose have aligned, and I am able to grow in every area of my life. Do that.

And then some:

1. Be consistent. Know that you have to commit time, money, energy and emotions to live within your passion and purpose.

2. Read books by experts in the field you wish to pursue.

3. Be adaptable. Welcome and expect change. I often think the Universe looks at our plans and laughs. When change is needed, learn to go along with it. Welcome it like a friend, and let go of the fear of change. So often people get stuck in the way it was always done, because it worked well in the past. Consider that there may be a way that it can work even better.

4. Surround yourself with like-minded people whom you trust. These are not 'yes' people; they are people who genuinely care about you.

5. Stop telling yourself stories that scare you. Censor other people's stories as well so that you are not taking on their fears or negative beliefs.

6. Never expect more from other people than you are willing to do yourself.

7. To stay focused on your passion, match your vibration to what you want.

SECTION FIVE

YOUR SPIRITUALITY: PRACTICE IT YOUR WAY

CHAPTER 23

A LIFE WITHOUT COMPARISON
(I'm feeling so spiritual right now.)

"Everything is perfect, until it is compared to something else."
Gregg Braden

Being human has its challenges. While the rest of the world (according to social media) is out and about living their life, riding their unicorn from yoga to the organic market, I am stuck in my humanness longing for a spiritual experience. Somehow in the midst of all of my enlightenment, there are still days when I think the only spiritual experience I will have today might be a cocktail.

My inner conflict is because I keep trying to resist my humanness. It keeps showing up, puffed-up ego and all, ready to pounce. I know, I know, we are not supposed to be judgmental, critical, or resentful. I try really hard to let things go, I really do, but c'mon, how many times do I have to go through this? Oh yeah, I remember now—until I learn the lesson.

In my twenties and thirties, I noticed a particular type of woman. They basically had the same haircut, same highlights and lowlights, same skirt, and same off-handed air of superiority about them. I noticed how they cut people with words, so I avoided them. Then I moved into my forties and noticed members of an elite society where they all spoke spiritual language, survived on nuts and seeds (but only the ones with healthy fats), and did 6,000 consecutive days of hot yoga. This time, I tried to gain membership into the elite club by learning to speak their language. Words like *releasing, mantra, afterlife, consciousness, dharma, spirit guides* and *third-eye* were tossed around like I had been using them my whole life. Did I believe the words? Absolutely! Did I enjoy being part of the club? Absolutely—until I started seeing the gap between the words and the actions.

I aged gracefully into my fifties, and noticed that the words, even when spoken with a smile and a sing-song voice, did not always align with the actions of the new and improved self-appointed guru. (Fun fact: the feminine is technically gurvi!)

The bob-sporting, skirt-wearing woman is child's play for the Gurvi hunter. This spiritual warrior can take you down with words in two sentences flat and have you believe it is your fault. They stand with their inflated bobblehead balanced on a pair of too-high wedged heels, with their bow pulled tight and carefully aimed, sharpened arrows dripping in niceness and spirituality. My bitchy self wants to knock that avatar flat on her vegan gluten-free ass. My spiritual self says, let it go. My real self will settle for somewhere in the middle, letting it go while not being disappointed if she twists her ankle and falls off her wedged pedestals all on her own.

These are the thoughts that run through my head as I supposedly reach for my highest level of spiritual consciousness. And you know what? It's okay. I don't need to be perfect all the time; I just need to be authentic and perfectly me. I aspire to remain in a state of balance and to surround myself with people who are the same—sometimes messy, sometimes enlightened, and always real.

Then there are times that I make up a story in my mind, further separating myself from my spiritual community. This happened to me a year ago when I agreed to go with three of my best like-minded girlfriends to a spiritual growth training event, adding on a few extra days for shopping and to hit the local bookstores.

Everything was good between us until the third night. Everyone was winding down and doing their own thing, talking on the phone, reading, and organizing their purchases. I was feeling tired but told them if they decided to go out to a lounge or late dinner to let me know and I would come along. Shortly after I went to my bedroom, I heard the door to the suite close with a lot of hushed laughter. I went out to the main living room and realized that they had left, and I was alone.

What I imagined: I was instantly transported back to

feelings of being *less than*. I felt excluded and rejected. I concluded that they must have decided to wait until I had gone to bed so they could sneak off and go do something fun without me. The next day my reaction was to brush them off and keep to myself, spending most of my time in my room watching old sitcom re-runs. When we all went for dinner later that night, I was polite but very quiet and not engaged. The morning after that, I did not even want to gather in the kitchen for coffee because I had convinced myself that I was not wanted and was cramping their style.

What probably happened: I am not a smoker and my friends are. Likely they were enjoying hanging out and waited until I went to bed for them all to go downstairs and have a few cigarettes outdoors. They probably took a drink with them and that is why they were laughing when they left.

What my friends think happened: Nothing. They probably have no idea that I was feeling hurt or left out.

What I did to resolve the situation: Nothing. My need to feel included and part of something, no matter how mature I get, hasn't gone away. Those old wounds still check in once in a while, just to see if I have released their power over me.

Creating separation—real or imagined—is what keeps us in competition with each other. It doesn't seem to matter how spiritual or evolved we think we are; we are still susceptible to our old patterns when we compare ourselves to others. I had concluded that I was not one of the group and was left out of something fun. Ironically, I know that in many circles I *am* the fun one (it's true), yet I easily slipped back into the messages from my childhood of not feeling wanted. I didn't need the Gurvi hunter to take me down—I had done it to myself.

The truth is we know when we are out of alignment and off balance. It feels uncomfortable, there are a thousand butterflies about to break loose from our ribcage, and we can't show up with love. The little voice in our head calls us a fraud when we talk about abundance and gratitude after spending the last hour (or week) in judgment and resentment. It is easy to remember what state of mind feels best both physically and mentally.

When we show up as we are—perceived flaws and all— we are free to shine our light. No one else's. Ours. Imagine living a life without comparison, fully embracing who we are. Imagine kicking the old beliefs we have about how we 'should' be to the curb. We could live authentically. We could be the lighting director in our own movie. We could choose to crank that dial fully on and shine our brightest, knowing that we are perfect just the way we are, right here, right now, no matter what is going on around us. We could choose to dim the light and spend some time in the shadows, resting, exploring our feelings, using the shade to provide cover when we feel we need it. We could choose to truly live as the best version of ourselves. Do that.

And then some:

1. Know that you are enough. Repeat this over and over throughout the day.

2. Stop all self-criticism. Now. This includes your thoughts.

3. Have daily positive conversations with yourself in the mirror. Know that you don't have to be anyone else's perception of you. You are perfect just the way you are. While you are at the mirror, repeat some positive affirmations to stretch your belief system.

4. Forgive yourself for the months, years or decades you spent trying to be someone else. The past is over. The future is yours to shine in—as you. (See Chapter 25 for more action steps on learning to forgive yourself.)

5. Stop comparing yourself to others. Just stop. You are the star of this show. The spotlight is right where it should be. On you.

CHAPTER 24

BELIEVE IN SOMETHING GREATER THAN YOURSELF

(You can't do it wrong, no matter what you have been led to believe.)

As you know by now, positive affirmations increase your self-belief and can help in ways that you may not realize at first. It might seem uncomfortable to you right now to repeat things that you know are not your current reality. Study after study has proven the benefit of positive affirmations in creating a new reality. Believing in something you can't see is an effective way to learn to believe in a power or force that is greater than yourself, and even more, connects us all together.

Growing your belief muscle takes practice. Here are some suggestions to help you bulk up! These are tools that will help you no matter what culture, religion or belief system you feel connected to.

Name one thing you are good at or have accomplished. For example, if you got out of bed today, that might be an achievement for you. If you spent time in nature, with friends, helping others or staying organized and that is important to you—then that is an achievement. If you completed something that you started—or had the wisdom to leave it behind you—that is an accomplishment. Maybe it is something regarding self-care. Did you take time to sit and relax with your coffee? That, too, is an accomplishment! If you feel good about it and it feels like an achievement, write it down in your journal.

Remind yourself of your worth and that you are a good person. Whatever that means to you, being a good person is important to feeling connected and part of society. It's important to tell yourself that you're a good person every single day. Make "I am a good person, I am enough" a part of your daily mantra.

Compile a list of things you want to be more focused on. Turn them into affirmations—personal, positive, present tense—and stretch your belief muscles by repeating them multiple times throughout the day. Ask for feedback from people you trust. Ask about your strengths, and focus on those positive traits. Use that feedback to build up your confidence. On days that you don't feel confident, this feedback can remind you of how powerful you really are.

As a child and even up into my twenties, when people complimented me, or enjoyed being my friend, employer or co-worker, I would think to myself, *If you knew who I really am, you wouldn't like me.* The real me had made so many mistakes she believed she was not lovable. I had absolutely no self-worth.

Years later, as I read books or have conversations with others, I find that most people have this imposter syndrome. No matter how successful people are, they can still feel like they don't deserve it. They feel as if everything they're doing is a fluke and at any moment someone else is going to find out about the truth. This was true for me almost every day of my life until I finally came around to believing that we are all the same and that there is a power greater than us that influences that likeness.

If you are feeling as if your success was too easy to come by compared to what you thought it would take before you experienced it, this can be a reason you experience imposter syndrome. You feel fraudulent because it was simple to achieve, and you now think it's not even that special because anyone can do it. The way to deal with this erroneous feeling is to look at some statistics. How many people in your situation have achieved what you have achieved? You're likely to find out that not as many people have succeeded doing what you're doing as you think. This information alone will help you realize that you had to be responsible at least a little for your achievement. Even if other people could do it if they wanted to—you did it, they did not.

If you are afraid it can all disappear overnight—you are right. But it is not likely going to happen so stop scaring yourself. Remind yourself of the history. You have been who you are for a long time. You have likely been doing what you are doing for a long time, including believing that you are an imposter. You are not. You are the real deal. This is just another way you convince yourself that you are *less than*, when you have been born *more than enough* and do not have to do anything to maintain that status. You are part of the greater whole and are deserving, perfect and lovable just because you exist.

You deserve the life you are building and it's okay to accept and value the things you have achieved. You could not have done it without making the choices you made. Even if you were given breaks, you chose what to do with them. Either way, you are where you are now due to your own choices at the time. You are valuable just by being who you are. Even if a million people are doing what you want to do, you provide a unique input and value to that thing that no one else can ever provide to your version of it. This means that even if you are making money selling blue jeans, which are everywhere, your jeans are special because you came up with the idea of selling them in your own unique way. Believe in yourself and it is easier to believe in the power of connection with each other and the universe.

Believing in yourself and others is key to your own spiritual growth—your way. To grow spiritually in a world defined by power, money, and influence takes daily commitment. It can be hard to find the balance between the material distractions, past beliefs, health, relationships and spiritual aspects of your life, but it can be done when you are willing to look inside.

We can also use our thoughts to believe in something greater than ourselves and utilise them to co-create beautiful life experiences. Our thoughts become our reality—here is an example of a situation where I used my thoughts and faith to co-create.

I was in San Diego, taking a course. My mother had passed two years earlier, and I wanted to acknowledge her birthday even though I was far from home. It was the last day of the conference and we were done at noon. I had arranged a late check-out and thought I would go to the ocean and think about my mother there before flying home. When I went to the hotel room to change my shoes, I realized how tired my body was and decided to honor myself by resting and meditating. I was able to release tension and feel the mental clarity for which I had been praying would come from the course.

I packed up and was ready to leave the room early, glad that I still had time to go to the ocean. The housekeeping supervisor knocked on my door and I told her I would be leaving momentarily. She was carrying a bouquet of white roses that a bride had left behind. After she left I thought about how nice it would be to have one of those roses to take to the ocean to release as a token of love to my mother. I only wished that they were red roses, as they were mom's favorite.

I summoned up the courage to ask the housekeeping supervisor if I could have one rose from the bouquet. I came upon her a couple of doors down carrying a smaller bouquet of roses, and imagine my surprise that this time they were red! I remembered my mission and asked for a single red rose. Instead, she insisted I take the whole bouquet of twelve beautiful long-stemmed red roses. After thanking her profusely, I knew just what to do. I checked out, stowed my bags, and headed for the beach.

I walked a bit further to where the beach was less populated. I began the process of dismantling the bouquet to make sure that I would only be putting organic matter into the ocean, all the while quietly singing *Happy Birthday* with the roar of the waves as my accompaniment. I waded out knee deep in the ocean. When I felt the time was right, I threw the roses into the ocean. Petals scattered, and then guided by the current they came back and floated all around me, creating a beautiful scene for my enjoyment. After a few minutes, I waded out of the water and headed back up the beach. I kept hearing the message in my mind, *Don't look back.* I wanted to look back and make sure everything was still as beautiful as I had left it, but I listened to the message.

Our belief in something greater than ourselves is an act of faith and self-love. Sometimes our beliefs and thoughts are about small everyday things; other times they are monumental and life altering.

Using introspection for spiritual growth goes beyond recalling the things that happened in a day, week, or month. We need to look closely and reflect on our thoughts, feelings, beliefs and motivations. Periodically examining our experiences, the decisions we make, the relationships we have, and the things we engage in provides useful insights about our life goals and our natural tendencies. Moreover, introspection gives us clues on how to act, react, and conduct ourselves in the midst of any situation. Like any skill, introspection can be learned; all it takes is the courage and willingness to seek the truths that lie within us. In order to do this, we must be forgiving of ourselves, and love ourselves first. Only then can we focus on forgiving others and building sustainable relationships.

It is all part of kicking the imposter mentality to the curb and not only accepting but embracing just how valuable we really are. To grow spiritually is to develop our potential and believe in ourselves. Beliefs, values, morality, rules, experiences, and good works provide the blueprint to ensure the growth of the spiritual being. To grow spiritually is to recognize interconnections.

Spiritual growth may not be our favorite topic, but if we look at things from a different point of view, we might have greater chances of enjoying the whole process instead of counting the days until we are fully improved and 'done' with our spiritual growth. I hear this from people regularly. They want to know when they will be finished, or they proudly declare that they finished their spiritual growth a long time ago. Both of these scenarios are incorrect. We are never done. We never arrive. And you can thank whatever higher power you believe in for that!

Maslow's hierarchy of needs identifies several human needs: physiological, safety, love/belonging, esteem, self-actualization, and transcendence. The James-Lange theory of emotion earlier categorized these needs into three: material, emotional, and spiritual. When we have satisfied the basic physiological and emotional needs, spiritual or existential needs come next. Achieving each need leads to the total development of the individual. Growth is a process, thus to grow in spirit is a day-to-day encounter. We win some, we lose some, but the important thing is that we learn, and from this knowledge, further spiritual growth is made possible. Whatever your something greater is—use it to achieve self-actualization and serve the world in your highest capacity. Do that.

And then some:

1. Silence the negative messages when they show up. You are not an imposter. When you have a negative thought, say, "Hello, thank you for sharing" and move on. Do not let that voice go on and on. Shut it down. Do something that requires thought and movement. Focus only on your feet hitting the ground, the sun on your skin, the water around you

or whatever it takes to reconnect you with who you really are.

2. Connect with like-minded people. Give them a call, plan a date, or send them a funny pic on Snapchat. Do whatever you can think of to get your positive thoughts flowing.

3. Do something for someone else. One way to overcome any type of negative self-talk or lack of connection is to go help someone else.

4. Do things that lift your mood and vibration. Turn up the music! Turn it up loud so that you can't help but sing and dance. Experiment with movement. When you change your physiology, you change your mindset.

5. Learn to give and receive compliments with grace. If you think you don't like receiving negative feedback, how do you feel about positive feedback? Does it make you squirm? There really is only one right way to deal with positive feedback—say, "Thank you very much." Allow the other person the gift of giving.

6. Strive to grow through introspection. Know that when something shows up that is not in alignment with your beliefs, it is a gem to help you learn. You can choose to notice it and move forward all while being thankful for the test and strengthening of your beliefs.

CHAPTER 25

PRACTICING FORGIVENESS
(And sometimes it takes a lot of practice.)

There is always going to be personal suffering when we do not forgive. Let me give you an example. My client Vanessa was once cheated on by her husband. Well, once that she knows of. She went forward in her life and appeared to have moved on. In her childhood, she had formed the belief that men could not be trusted, and her belief was reinforced by this failed relationship. She became angry and aggressive within her new relationships. Because she held onto the anger, she sabotaged relationships that could have worked out well for her. Before men were able to prove their love for her, her anger made her act in a way that actually drove them away.

Vanessa found herself going through the pockets of her new partner. She found herself looking for problems even if there were none because she was unable to accept that people could be good to her. By doing so, she diminished herself and made herself less desirable as a partner.

If Vanessa had looked at the situation from a different perspective, she would have been able to find forgiveness. Let me be clear here—the forgiveness is for her own healing and does not condone what her husband did. If she had chosen forgiveness instead of bitterness, she would have created a better future for herself. In time, she would have been able to free herself from all of the negative emotions she was feeling. Instead she remained stuck in her story, blaming others, and refusing to use the negative experience as a tool to help her grow emotionally. It was much easier to be the victim, until it wasn't.

I remember being wronged by someone in a way so severe it impacted my entire family. I was clearly the victim and wore the banner for a good ten years. Who am I kidding?—it was closer to twenty. In the beginning I would lay in bed at night wishing harm on the other people involved. Believe it or not, it helped the pain of the moment subside and I was able to get some sleep. After the need for revenge subsided, I was able to pick up the pieces and move on. But I never forgave, and I certainly never forgot. Twenty years later, and many years into my spiritual path, I finally got to the place where I was willing to look at forgiveness. It was hard to do because the wounded part of me wanted an apology that I knew I was never going to get,

When we cannot forgive, we imprison ourselves rather than the person we cannot forgive. We suffer from anger, hate, negativity, lack of trust and all of the things that make us feel *less than*. From a very young age, we form our behavior based on years of interaction with others, which includes our family, friends, teachers, neighbors, and perceived interactions.

I perceived at a very young age that it was best to numb my feelings. I did it through most of my childhood and then into my adult life. It was a way for me to protect myself from hurt and become untouchable. I lashed out as another form of self-protection. I believed if I could hurt the other person, they would not get a chance to do it to me. As I matured and was in my mid-twenties, I was able to recognize this behavior and shift it. I didn't have the skills to make it go away entirely, but after a lot of adjusting my 'trust levels' I was able to navigate in a less sabotaging way. This is something that I have had to learn to forgive myself for so that I don't continue to carry it forward into each stage of my life. Man, I thought learning how to forgive others was hard; learning to forgive myself was even harder.

In order to forgive myself I had to thaw the numbed feelings and acknowledge the ways that I had taken part in the many hurts in my life. I had to accept responsibility for them and make regular efforts to not return to the old patterns of numbing, shutting down or lashing out.

We can choose to use all the past painful experiences and failures as a positive reinforcement to improve ourselves.

Forgiving others and moving on not only releases us from the negative emotions but strengthens our confidence in overcoming obstacles that we all face in one way or another. Learn from experience and move on. It is hard, but it is worth it. When we do that, we practice our right to choose how to respond—rather than react —and we become champions of our own happiness.

Getting back to Vanessa's experience, she managed to grow in character after being alone for a while. She realized that she held grudges both against her cheating husband for treating her like dirt as if she had no worth—and against herself because she hadn't lived up to his expectations.

After a long struggle, she was surprised that she was able to forgive him. It made her feel whole again. It was like walking away with her head held high. She used empathy to try and see the situation from her husband's viewpoint, bearing in mind the way he was raised and his low self-esteem. That doesn't mean that she called him to give him the green light and declare her forgiveness. She simply forgave and continued to work on herself. Vanessa had a lot of negative feelings about herself to resolve because she recognized how she could have handled things differently within the marriage. Even while they were together, she resented him and made no effort to hide it. She was pushing him away without ever verbalizing it. Even though she is not responsible for his actions, Vanessa became willing to be responsible for her own.

As she went through the healing process, Vanessa found that she had to let go of her past and move on as the past does not equal the future. Today, she has been able to form a strong foundation in her life and now enjoys a loving relationship with mutual respect and love.

My life was one abusive relationship after another because I never formed my relationship with self. I numbed out anything I didn't want to see or hear and kept my focus on what was working. Sounds like a great strategy, right? It is for a while, but eventually I could no longer numb out what was unacceptable to me and I would have yet another relationship end.

I had to learn to love myself enough to forgive myself and to accept myself as is—a work in progress yet *more than enough*. When I did this, I become the person that I was comfortable being without all of my numbing tools of denial, addiction, and self-protection. I learned how to approach life from a much more compassionate viewpoint for myself and for others. It turns out that not all people were out to hurt me, and that many really could be trusted. Now I am surrounded by so many people who truly love me for being me, and that could not have happened until I learned to love, accept, and forgive myself.

To do that, I practiced meditation and self-reflection. The interesting part of meditation is that it teaches you how to let go of all thoughts and to give them no credence. As you ponder upon your life, you are subjected to all kinds of opinions. Thoughts come and go, and you seem to have very little control over them. However, when you meditate, you need to focus on your breathing. If your thoughts wander, you acknowledge the thoughts and simply let them go without allowing your emotions to take over. At the same time, you're practicing the principle of non-judgment. After all, it's just a thought and that's all there is to it. Of course, it's easier said than done. But in meditation, you simply focus on your breathing.

In my opinion, meditation can be done anytime and anywhere—you will learn your way for yourself. Here is a method to get you started:

Sit on a chair that gives you plenty of support. It's best to use a dining chair rather than something that you sink into, because the straightness of your back is important. Your feet should remain flat and planted onto the floor. Your hands, palms up and open, are placed on your lap. Keeping your back straight, breathe in but instead of only using the top of your lungs like people normally do, breathe in extra deeply until you feel the air in your upper gut. Hold onto it for a moment and then breathe out. You continue in this way, counting to 5 for the inhale, holding for 5, and counting to 5 for the exhale. Exhale until your lungs are completely empty. Do this slowly—it should not sound like you are about to hyperventilate nor should you feel like you are going to pass out. Eventually, the counting will become unnecessary as you relax and sink into the process of meditation.

During this exercise, your mind is busy with counting and concentrating on the breath, so you don't have time to think about anything else. This is the bit that people find difficult, but that is why it is suggested that you practice meditation twenty minutes a day and make meditation part of your lifestyle. Practice helps to discipline the mind. If you notice that there are thoughts popping up in your mind, realize that it's normal. Don't resist them. Simply observe them. See them, acknowledge that they are there and then let them go.

Let's face it. When we are hurt or angry, it is not going to be easy to sit and meditate. Feelings are influenced by our thoughts and perceptions. Denying our feelings often leads to depression and anxiety. It is normal to experience a wide range of feelings including jealousy, hatred, frustration, irritation and other negative emotions. They exist to guide us. There is no need to blame ourselves for these feelings, because we will only create even more negative emotions. We get more of what we focus on. However, we can always reach for our next highest emotion.

Esther Hicks has been teaching the principles of the Law of Attraction since the 1980's. She has published an emotional guidance scale to help you reach for the next highest emotion. You can spiral up and down the scale depending on where you focus your energy. When you practice forgiveness, you will climb up the emotional guidance scale. When you focus on the negative—you guessed it—you get more of it. Accept that you feel what you feel and get ready to turn the negative energy into positive energy.

Emotional Guidance Scale – Abraham and Esther Hicks

1. Joy/Appreciation/Empowered/Freedom/Love
2. Passion
3. Enthusiasm/Eagerness/Happiness
4. Positive Expectation/Belief
5. Optimism
6. Hopefulness
7. Contentment
8. Boredom
9. Pessimism
10. Frustration/Irritation/Impatience
11. Overwhelmed
12. Disappointment
13. Doubt
14. Worry
15. Blame
16. Discouragement
17. Anger

18. Revenge

19. Hatred, Rage

20. Jealous

21. Insecurity/Guilt/Unworthiness

22. Fear/Grief/Despair/Depression/Powerlessness

When we are learning to forgive either ourselves or someone else, we need to acknowledge the thoughts that we have and try to see them without all the emotions kicking in. Then let them go and reach for a higher feeling on the Emotional Guidance Scale. When we free ourselves from being caught up in situations and emotions, we experience inner peace. Do that.

And then some:

1. When you have decided to forgive someone, there is no reason to bring up the past again. Absolute forgiveness means that you are able to put all of that behind you and move on.

2. When you forgive yourself, practice the same principle. Do not replay your old stories and relive the negative emotions attached to it. Use breathwork and meditation to truly release any negative feelings you have about yourself.

3. Learn to see things differently. Consider them from all angles. If you are holding preconceived ideas about why a situation worked out the way it did, practice looking at things with an open mind. When

you do this, you broaden the spectrum of your understanding, and life will go a lot smoother for you, no matter what happens around you.

4. If you are able to forgive, it empowers you so much that everything seems so positive and you are able to go through life with a whole new viewpoint. We're all human beings. We all make mistakes. We all go through peaks and valleys. However, when you learn to make forgiveness part of the way you live, the weight of burden will lighten and disappear.

5. Consider learning to be a more tolerant person. Learn all about other religions and other races to broaden the spectrum of your life and be able to put things into perspective. If you don't have an understanding of why things are the way they are, perhaps you can have compassion. When you learn to forgive, you become more compassionate. And when you become more compassionate, you learn to forgive. Do you see how that works? Compassion can lead you down the path of peace and healing. You learn to let go of your preconceived beliefs and move on.

6. Forgiveness is an important part of a full and healthy life. It enables you to begin to build a foundation for your life. A foundation built upon negative thoughts is like building a house in quicksand. You can't do it. If you continue to walk through your life without forgiving yourself for the things that you have done

wrong, you carry all of that burden with you. If you learn to forgive, you build a solid foundation that can help people around you to trust who you are. Please, if you do nothing else in this book, work on forgiving yourself and others. It is the only way to set yourself free from the past and to be the person you were put on this earth to be.

CHAPTER 26

GRATITUDE CHANGES EVERYTHING
(And everything changes with gratitude.)

Gratitude is seeing life as a gift you get to open each day. Once you feel great about the world and about your life, no matter what the circumstance, you will find peace. It can be hard to maintain a state of gratitude when it feels like everything is going wrong, but if you remain thankful you will eventually see the hidden blessings in everything. I'm talking about feeling gratitude in the unexpected moments, not just when things are going well. This is not a state of false happiness; it is just a way of living that helps you to be in alignment with your desires.

We often think of gratitude as something we need to express after we have experienced what we want. We experience something that we want, and we are grateful or at minimum say thank you. What if we expressed gratitude for the things we desire, believing that everything we desire is trying to make its way to us even if we can't see it, not even on the horizon? What if we could feel what it would be like to have what we desire before we have it? Many people believe that being in alignment with our desires helps us manifest from a place where we have the power to achieve our desires.

Start from where you are. This can apply to all the different areas of your life. You can practice gratitude now. There are no prerequisites. Take a moment to look around where you are. What are you experiencing? What in your surroundings can you find to be grateful for? How is your body feeling? Did you automatically do a mental body scan looking for any aches and pains, or did you thank your legs for supporting you and your eyes for allowing you to see?

We have been conditioned to think that it is only acceptable to feel good when things are flowing just how we want them to be. Then, when things are not as we think they should be, we set our gratitude aside and reserve our happiness and good vibes for another time. By repeating this practice on a daily basis, we are literally deteriorating our quality of life using only our state of mind.

Instead, we can choose to follow a path to a happy and joyous life by deciding irreversibly—no matter what, no matter who, no matter when or how—that we will choose to be grateful and mindfully stay in a state of happiness. I'm not talking about fake-smile-pasted-on happy. I'm talking about deep happiness even if what you are experiencing in the moment is pain or loss. Are you confused yet? I get it. It can be confusing. Stay with me here, and trust the process.

What I am suggesting is that gratitude and happiness run deeper than the emotion of the moment. Gratitude and happiness are your natural state of being that allow you to connect to your source and therefore to exactly who you are. All that you have to do is reach for the feeling, and there it is. It may take a little self-exploration, but your true self is in there and wants to express its light. Look at young children and how they appreciate the simplest of things; that is who you are when you allow yourself to connect to your natural state of gratitude.

When I go to bed at night, I visualize my day and offer thoughts of gratitude. Then I visualize the day to come and do the same. Usually that process continues on throughout the night in dreams, feelings and thoughts. When I awaken, I am usually in a positive frame of mind. Occasionally, that is not the case. I recently woke up to unwelcome noises and was irritable before I even opened my eyes. As I lay in bed, I prepared mini-speeches that expressed my unhappiness. When my sanity returned, I realized that the magpies and crows would not have cared about my well-thought-out speech, so I refrained from wandering into the yard to verbalize my feelings.

I carried my mood throughout the morning. I muttered complaints to myself about people who don't clean up after themselves, and drivers that do not use their signal lights. I concluded it was just going to be one of those days. And that is where I caught myself.

Once I recognized that I was out of alignment with who I really am, it became easier to offer gratitude for the simple things surrounding me—the trees that held the noisy birds, their different shades of green, and even the majestic grace and beauty of the magpies and crows. Well, their appearance anyway—their sound was still like nails on a chalkboard to me. I began to be grateful for the city planners who ensured that green space was maintained. I became aware of the sunshine, the clean water, and that safe place where I live. This went on for the rest of the day and what started out as a rough day quickly became a day of appreciation.

What changed? Only my thoughts. Some days controlling my thoughts is effortless; some days it is easier to give in to the negativity. We all have a variety of feelings to deal with. The Law of Attraction states "that which is like unto itself is drawn." When we find ways to live in gratitude no matter what our outside circumstances are, we will draw more things into our life to be appreciative and grateful for.

Our setbacks make us stronger. Forgive yourself first. Forgive everyone involved (even if that means in mind only) and return to a state of well-being as quickly as possible. We do not want to draw more turmoil or pain into our lives by continuing to live in a low vibration state. Choosing to live in a negative state pushes positive emotions away and does not allow them to pass through us. We become stuck and the negativity grows into jealousy, resentment and anger. Alternatively, when we choose to release the negativity and reach for higher thoughts of gratitude, appreciation and trust, by the very nature of the higher-vibration thought, we draw more opportunities to be thankful for.

Being grateful in any kind of situation is a powerful and strong attracting force. Gratitude reduces negativity, helps people learn, improves relationships and most importantly, gratitude attracts the things that you want. This is a universal and powerful force that changes lives.

Once we find things we appreciate and put emphasis on the things we are thankful for, we create space for more goodness in our lives. If we are in a state of gratitude, we are also in a high energy vibration, which is essential to attracting more things that we can be thankful for. With all the positive characteristics of gratitude, it is really hard for anyone to find any disadvantage about it. Naysayers accuse those who practice gratitude of having their head in the clouds and not seeing the negativity right in front of them. To those people I say, thank you, thank you very much. But seriously, as important as it is to be aware of what is happening in every aspect of our life, it is entirely our decision to choose what to focus on.

When we find a way to be grateful for our imperfections, we can appreciate the opportunity to improve. We learn more about who we are as people when we are in the practice of high-vibration self-improvement. Every challenge is a lesson that helps to develop our character. When we show our gratitude to everyone and to every situation, we see how it can change our quality of life and improve the lives of those around us. Do that.

And then some:

1. Read through the meditation included in the Appendix of this book. Read it often and find what is working in your life and what needs to be healed. Be grateful for them both.

2. Count your blessings. Practice thankfulness for the little things. Notice the simple pleasures in life.

3. Live life like it is one big miracle, being fully aware of the blessings that surround you.

4. Make a practice of shifting your focus from lack to abundance. Not only will you be happier, but you will also be healthier. Being in a state of love improves your immune system and reduces stress.

5. It has been proven that most people stay trapped in the financial class that they are born into. Practicing gratitude attracts abundance and can help you break free toward financial freedom. There is always something more to count when you are counting your blessings. If you want $1,000 but only have $100, be thankful for each and every dollar that makes up the money that you have.

6. Become mindful about the beauty around you— green grass, butterflies, even rainy days! Celebrate the

food on your table and your good health. Acknowledge them as blessings, and your life will become happier.

7. Develop a daily gratitude practice that includes others. In my home, we hold hands at dinner and talk about what we are thankful for. If we have company, the ritual stays in place. It is good for us, and it is good for others to participate in and hopefully be inspired to start a gratitude practice of their own.

CHAPTER 27

YOU GET MORE OF WHATEVER YOU FOCUS ON

(So stop focusing on what you don't want—and put ALL your focus on what you DO WANT!)

"If you believe it will work out, you'll see opportunities. If you believe it won't, you will see obstacles."
Dr. Wayne Dyer

I have been blessed with having many wonderful mentors and spiritual teachers in my life. One of the most impactful was Dr. Wayne Dyer. He and Louise Hay taught me that you really do get more of what you focus on. If you focus on health, negative or positive, you get more of that.

Both of my parents were pure superstars in this regard. They both had cancer and absolutely refused to be victim to it. My mother completely convinced herself that she was cancer-free and died at home from what we assume was a stroke or heart attack four years after we were told she had only six months to live. My father always said that he was a miracle man. I smile just remembering the words. He refused to be a victim of the disease and kept his thoughts and words positive until he was just too tired and drifted off with his final breath at eighty-nine years old. Whatever you focus on determines the quality of your life. My parents focused on the blessings, healing, and miracles that they believed would be their truth—and they were.

Dr. Wayne Dyer is considered as 'the father of motivation,' and his enlightened understanding made him a friend to all of humankind. Over the last few weeks I have been re-reading some of his books as a way to fully appreciate the man who spent his life teaching people about self-reliance and spiritual awareness. My favorite book authored by him is *I Can See Clearly Now*.

He followed no particular world religion or teaching, but rather followed them all. He often mentioned his most influential teachers as Rumi, St. Francis of Assisi, Jesus, Buddha, Krishna, Lao Tzu, and many more. He didn't focus on his teacher's differences, but rather on their similarities of giving, love, and oneness.

One of my favorites of his quotes is: "When you change the way you look at things, the things you look at change." I have found this to be a go-to mantra in my life. If I am in a place of conflict or fear, often by just repeating this thought in my mind, I can shift to a clearer and more productive perspective. This way, when life presents me with a challenge, I can keep an open mind, give up my personal agenda (ego) and let Divine providence work on my behalf.

In his memoir, *I Can See Clearly Now*, he wrote about his life experiences, things that for many people would have been absolute crises. Repeatedly throughout the book, a chapter, or even a page, he used the phrase 'I can see clearly now that ...' this challenge needed to happen because when I look back I can see how I got where I am ... how things would have been different ... and how I wouldn't have had the opportunities or people that I have in my life now. After reading this uplifting book I was inspired to journal some of my own experiences, and how I can see clearly now why things needed to happen in a certain way for me.

It is an exercise that I am encouraging you to do as well. Recognize the Divine order of your life. Even if it feels chaotic, there is a higher agenda at work. For me, journaling was an opportunity to give up my personal history and the things that I perceived as negative, and to release them with thankfulness. With this new perspective I can offer forgiveness and acceptance both to myself and to the other people who have influenced my life along the way. Had I not taken those steps, this book would have never been written.

I have learned that journal reflection is an important part of discovering my own personal path of enlightenment, which is another reason why I am encouraging you to do the same. Remember, when you change the way you look at things, the things you look at change.

Another book that proves that focus determines quality of life is Dr. Wayne Dyer's book, *You'll See it When you Believe It.* Through the lessons in this book I have been encouraged to be fearless with my dreams and imagination. I have repeatedly observed (in awe) that when I become clear on an outcome, the outcome manifests for me. I have been careful not to set tight parameters, but instead to trust that everything always works out for my highest good and on its own timeline.

I believe that every moment of my existence holds an infinite number of possibilities. My job is to get out of the way and allow the Universe to conspire in my favor! As long as I have a willingness to listen to my inner voice— my true self, my soul—I can go anywhere and do anything and simply allow any success to come to me. Isn't that exciting? It is true for each of us.

I urge you to do the same things that he has taught me to do. Be loving yet compassionate, fearless yet aware, humble yet magnificent. A few years ago, I wrote the affirmation, *I release the patterns in my consciousness that are creating resistance to my good. I deserve to feel good.* Since then, I have had the courage to leave both a relationship and a career that no longer served my best interest, repaired relationships with my family and friends, multiplied my income several times and attracted my soul mate to whom I am now engaged! Repeating my affirmation helps me to focus on my good, creating even more good in my life.

The things that we resist are an illusion. Think of a young child who is scared of the dark. All fears dissipate when the bedroom light is turned on. The monster under the bed is just an illusion hiding in the dark.

Our fears, focus, and distraction hide in more places than the dark. Sometimes they hide in our addictions. Sometimes we need to let go of what is normal to us so that we can determine what we would like to focus on.

A few years ago, I sat down at my computer and typed a chapter heading. Then half an hour passed while I checked all of my several accounts on my phone. Apparently, the fact that I had done that twice already that morning, and there were no notifications of new email was irrelevant. I still needed to check. The fact that I was not waiting for any particular email was also a trivial detail that I ignored while I scrolled through the promotions folder of my Gmail. I lost interest and set the phone down. Next to my computer was my iPad. I use it for reference checking as I write.

On the screen the Facebook tab caught my eye. I saw the number one in parentheses, so I knew at least someone out there liked something I'd said or maybe they had updated their status with a cute picture. I had to check it out. What if it was important? What if it would make me feel important, or warm and fuzzy? It turned out it was someone selling something and I begrudgingly hit the 'X' that makes the Facebook tab disappear from my screen. My next thought was food. I had a quick snack and got back to writing. Thankfully, I had my cable disconnected or you may have never been reading this book!

The irony is that one of my most favorite things to do is to write. I love to create, to watch the words come together in a way that feels sacred to me and both entertains and inspires my readers. If I get quiet the words find their way to the page. They are often accompanied by tears. Sometimes dainty streams leak from my eyes, and sometimes guttural sobs erupt as I release all that I've been harboring inside of me. So why all the distractions? Because getting real means getting vulnerable. It takes courage to will myself to face whatever needs to find its way to the blank page.

The same is true whether our distraction is technology, chronic over-doing, indulging in alcohol, over-eating, or another addiction. When we quiet our distractions, our feelings get louder, and we are left to face them without our defensive weapon of choice. We are left to face our true feelings and to find the courage to overcome them just as we are.

I remember a story that Dr. Wayne Dyer loved to tell about how when you squeeze an orange you get orange juice. His point was that when you are under pressure, your real self emerges.

A few years ago, I suffered through three deaths in my immediate family. I am not a person who uses the word 'suffer' lightly, but for me, there is no other word to describe the pain I felt. I had lost my youngest sister tragically, and my mother, both within a ten-month period. My father-in-law passed three months later. I coped by doing. I made sure everything was arranged and as it should be. I took care of people and details, all the while lulling myself to sleep at night with medication, the television, and my laptop simultaneously. Anything that could distract me from thinking was a welcome diversion.

Then I was forced to unplug. I had made a commitment to go meet my then-husband in Mexico where he had been on a soul-searching mission of his own. We went out to a secluded beach with a reef to do some snorkeling. The world got quiet. I started to cry, which was challenging in both the goggles and the mouthpiece of the snorkel, but somehow, I managed. My painful expression contorted and hidden, my salty tears mixing with the sea.

I spotted a large turtle and just watched, my tears releasing, my soul absorbing the magnificence. Soon a second turtle joined alongside the first, followed by two large yellow fish. The yellow fish swam so close to the turtle that I was afraid they were hurting her. As I

211

continued to watch I noticed they were eating off of her shell and using her to rest upon. The turtle was eating too.

She swam up to the surface and alongside me, plunging again, and then resurfacing for another visit. I became overwhelmed by this simple gesture. I thought of my mother, and how she was so afraid of new things. I felt like I brought her with me and that she could see the turtles, too. In fact, she could see everything clearly now and without fear.

I swam in close enough to touch the bottom. With the soft sand under my toes, I stood facing the vast ocean and cried openly. I cried tears of sorrow and tears of joy. Once I composed myself, I turned to face the beach. Anchored not twenty feet from me was a quaint little fishing boat painted bright yellow. It was named *CHARLOTTE*, the name of my sister that had passed. It was magical, they were here with me, my wounds were healing, the suffering lessening.

A hurricane warning had been issued for later in the day. It was in the stillness of the edge of the storm that I found my healing. Winds of change. Calm waters, rough waters, facing my fears to see what I so desperately wanted clarity in. I learned to look inside of myself for the answers, because everything I need is right there inside me. I learned to trust in the process even when I couldn't see the end game. What I could see were all of the blessings in my life. I put my focus on the horizon, far beyond the rough waters. Do that.

And then some:

Louise Hay's purpose was to help people to love themselves more. For the final *& Then Some* in this book, I am sharing Louise's clear steps on how to love yourself.

1. Stop all criticism. Criticism never changes a thing. Refuse to criticize yourself. Accept yourself exactly as you are. Everybody changes. When you criticize yourself, your changes are negative. When you approve of yourself, your changes are positive.

2. Forgive yourself. Let the past go. You did the best you could at the time with the understanding, awareness and knowledge that you had. Now you are growing and changing, and you will live life differently.

3. Don't scare yourself. Stop terrorizing yourself with your thoughts. It's a dreadful way to live. Find a mental image that gives you pleasure (author insertion: mine is yellow roses), and immediately switch your scary thought to a pleasure thought.

4. Be gentle and kind and patient. Be gentle with yourself. Be kind to yourself. Be patient with yourself as you learn the new ways of thinking. Treat yourself as you would someone you really loved.

5. Be kind to your mind. Self-hatred is only hating your own thoughts. Don't hate yourself for having the thoughts. Gently change the thoughts.

6. Praise yourself. Criticism breaks the inner spirit. Praise builds it up. Praise yourself as much as you can. Tell yourself how well you are doing with every little thing.

7. Support yourself. Find ways to support yourself. Reach out to friends and allow them to help you. It is being strong to ask for help when you need it.

8. Be loving to your negatives. Acknowledge you created them to fulfill a need. Now you are finding new, positive ways to fulfill those needs. So, lovingly release the old negative patterns.

9. Take care of your body. Learn about nutrition. What kind of fuel does your body need to have optimum energy and vitality? Learn about exercise. What kind of exercise do you enjoy? Cherish and revere the temple you live in.

10. Do mirror work. Look into your own eyes often. Express this growing sense of love you have for yourself. Forgive yourself while looking into the mirror. Talk to your parents while looking into the mirror. Forgive them, too. At least once a day say: "I love you, I really love you!"

11. LOVE YOURSELF ... DO IT NOW! Don't wait until you get well, or lose the weight, or get the new job, or find the new relationship. Begin NOW—and do the best you can.

12. Have Fun. Remember the things that gave you joy as a child. Incorporate them into your life now. Find a

way to have fun with everything you do. Let yourself express the joy of living. Smile. Laugh. Rejoice, and the Universe rejoices with you!

CONCLUSION

Like almost every personal development speaker and author, my desire is that my words have impacted your life in some way that is enough for you to take action. We all like to be inspired and motivated, but not much changes until we commit to action. When we take positive action, we change, and by that movement alone, the whole world changes for the better. Just imagine the global impact when we all do our part to be more honest, loving, thoughtful, respectful, and truthful human beings. I hope you have found what you need to take action between the covers of this book.

In order to have a transformational shift in your life, listen closely for what is calling you. And then take action. Live a brave life. By far, the scariest thing I have ever done is take the thoughts from my head and put the words on paper where I can't hide from them or take them back. I knew I needed to publish this book and that writing and helping people is my calling—my ministry. I became willing to risk the disapproval of others and trust myself. Be the person that you dream of being. You can start now; you do not have to wait. Leave unworthiness behind you.

Sometimes things happen in our lives that change us forever. We are impacted by circumstances that include tragedy, loss, fear and betrayal. If you have worked though this book and want help on the next steps, go to the resources page and contact my team for support.

I would also love to hear what you are healing in your life. How are you nurturing that inner child, improving your health, embracing your relationships, creating your best life on a day-to-day basis? Have you identified and claimed what your spiritual life means to you? If you feel inspired to share, please do.

Remember that it is not the right thing to do if it is not right for you. Listen for that inner guide and—rather than strive to reach your destination and *complete* the self-actualization process—let Divine wisdom lead you to the next step. People who have accomplished great things are often quoted as saying the most valuable or meaningful part was the journey and not the destination. Remember the saying, "Wherever you go, there you are." This is your journey. Do it your way, and do it while knowing that no matter what you experience along the way, you are worthy, you deserve to be loved, and you are *more than enough*.

ACKNOWLEDGMENTS

First and foremost, I would like to thank my friends and family for putting up with me as I went on the emotional roller coaster that came with the writing of this book. Oh, we have come this far, let's be honest, thank you for putting up with the roller coaster that has been my life! I am in the front row now, and instead of screaming or hiding my eyes, I am going forward with my eyes wide open. You helped me feel safe and supported enough to get here, so thank you. Mom and Dad, who have gone on to another place—that includes you. I am so thankful that you chose me.

To my birth family, thank you for understanding that I wrote this book through my own lens. I know your perception will be different than mine, and that is okay. We are family, and nothing changes that.

To my children. I have thought of you often while writing. For all of those times where I missed the mark as a parent, know that I have always known that you are *more than enough*. For those times when you felt like *less than*, I understand your pain, and I wish that you could see what I see in you. You are my most brilliant creations and I am so proud of you.

To my writing consultant and friend, Christy Dixon, thank you for so generously sharing your knowledge, and for helping me dig deeper when I wanted to keep my secrets buried. To my editor, Sheila Cameron, for tolerating my expectations and excelling through unrealistic deadlines. You were right—we both have *I can do it* attitudes, and together, we did it! Thank you!

Thank you to my friend Sandra Filer, who pointed out that I often *do that and then some*, inspiring the title of this book. Thank you to my friend Stacy Scriven, who never once in the last twenty-some years has said, "I told you so," even when we both knew you could have. I am thankful for each of you.

To my wonderful soulmate, Chris, you are truly the person I have been searching for my whole life. I have never felt more loved, safe, supported and protected as I do with you. You taught me that it is alright to want to feel that way, and to accept the love you have so generously given me. You have my heart for as long as it continues to beat in my chest. You allowed this book to be born. I don't know if I would have been brave enough without you. I love you.

APPENDIX

A GIFT FOR YOU – A GUIDED MEDITATION FOR INNER HEALING

Something More

Deep in the center of my mind, there is a place of pure love and everlasting peace. This place of beauty is whole, protected and easily accessible. In my minds' eye, I see a lake and trails that wind through the forest surrounding this body of water. I can enter this scene by reaching for a thought, sometimes for just a quick glimpse, other times for a limitless state of tranquility.

I am strong and grounded, understanding that everything good comes from love, and that I can return to love any time I choose. Taking a deep breath in, my mind is clearing the path to access my sanctuary. After exhaling completely, my lungs naturally draw in the pure air needed for my journey. Pausing everything else, I continue to breathe. I can now visualize the first glimpses of the place in my mind that embraces my natural haven. I can draw on this feeling wherever I am, and in whatever situation I may find myself. Standing at the top of the hill that leads down to the pathway, I am motionless. I continue to focus on my breathing, inhaling a slow deliberate expansion of my thoughts, exhaling any negativity that has been holding me back. I repeat this process until I feel like all the darkness I was storing has been released.

My breath is deep and intertwined with thoughts of pure gratitude. I am appreciative for all of the days of my life. I know that each moment has served me in some way. I remember that in every situation, I can choose to return to the lake, my quiet church. My place of reverence is only a thought away.

The branches of the trees display leaves that are bright with the colors of autumn. Bursts of green, red, orange and gold reach my vision before the calm, blue water that lies serenely behind the trees. The still water calls to me, reminding me of the stillness of my soul, renewing an assurance in my being that all is well in my world. When the sun is bright, diamonds appear to dance across the water, shimmering and vibrant. There is an awakening. My thoughts are alive and creative. These thoughts continue to transform, this time morphing into solid inspiration to guide me while fulfilling my life's purpose. Encouraged, I take a few more moments to focus on my breathing. I visualize in great detail all that I aspire to achieve in every area of my life. I visualize happiness and harmony for everyone close to me, and for those I will never meet. Holding myself in this place of service, I feel blessed. I know that it is in giving that I receive.

When the sun is hidden behind the clouds and the water appears gray, my thoughts turn inward for a time of deeper understanding and reflection. I recall a situation in my life where I would have chosen to respond differently. Examining this situation, I release all guilt and criticism, instead looking only for the lesson to help me better understand the circumstances. I think of the other people involved in this scenario, and I forgive them and release them. They were doing the best they could, with the understanding that they had at the time. This is a place for growing, a place for healing, and ultimately a

Thoughts of gratitude open my mind to hear the beautiful symphony of creative concepts, philosophies, and forgiveness that are always available to me, just a thought away.

As I come around a corner, the fog sits low on the water. I feel my deepest losses here but understand them with clarity. I am grateful to everyone who has shared in my life. Those who have passed on, or have simply passed through my life, are often with me in this place. I see signs of them in a turtle, or a heron, a butterfly, or a sky that is dark and low. I observe the way the small vines and willows cling to the more mature trees, wrapping themselves around the stronger tree for support and stability. It is here I remember that there have been times in my life when I have been the more mature tree and have used my roots to hold myself up and to encourage growth in others. I remember the times in my life when I was the willowy vine holding tightly onto those whom I believed to be stable, depending on them for what felt like my very survival, putting my trust in them. I remember both of these times with gratitude, knowing that all I have experienced in my life has been for my greatest good. Although I have been hurt and put my trust in those who did not always care for it as tenderly as I had intended, I know that each experience helped my roots to grow deeper. I became stronger, more resilient and less impacted by storms that approached and eventually passed by. I am deeply grounded in the knowledge of who I am and what is important in my life.

As I climb upward, the trails cut into the hill, and I reach the summit. This is a place where the sun is always shining, warming the massive dark-colored boulders that form the rock face to the water below. I sit on the dry, heated platform for a few minutes of silent meditation. Again, I focus on my breathing, absorbing the bright and powerful light of the Universe, and allowing it to flow through my body. I absorb inspiration and embrace an energy that is deeply insightful. Intuition flows freely as if the sunlight combines with the colors of the trees and the water, creating a prism of light that illuminates me from head to toe. This light opens up, clears each of my chakras, balances my soul. My eyes have been opened. The light is beckoning me to really see what life holds for me. It guides me to awaken, to know that everything I could ever desire is available to me, to know that I am enough just the way I am. I am perfect; I am ready to answer the call; I am willing. I continue to breathe in this healing light. I abandon all ego-based thinking, and my thoughts become as clear as the clean mountain water. My senses are on full alert, my vision and hearing no longer impaired by negativity. I hear nothing, and I hear everything. In the distance there is the whispering of something more that is building to a crescendo that can be heard by anyone who has opened their mind and heart to the call of serving others, all while living a gentle yet powerful life.

As I meander the winding shoreline I never have to search for my path. Somehow, I never lose my way as long as I keep moving forward. It is like the serene reflection on the lake resembles the quiet reflection occurring in my body, neither of us leading nor following. My mind and soul are faithfully trusting that I am continuously where I am intended to be, moving in the right direction, always safe, eternally protected.

My soul is full, overflowing with love and simple appreciation. I know that it is safe to give, because the supply of love knows no limits. I continue to advance on my journey, surrounded by faith, supported in the arms of everlasting love, strengthened by each step. And so it is.

Victoria Johnson

RESOURCES

For free resources from the author or information on *Do That & Then Some Companion Workbook,* visit www.victoriajohnson.org. or www.amazon.com

For more information on Heal Your Life® Training with Victoria Johnson, authorized by Hay House and approved by Louise Hay, visit www.thetraining.ca.

For more information on personality types, visit www.personalitydimensions.org.

For more information on coping stances by Virginia Satir, visit www.satirworkshops.com.

For most books mentioned in *Do That & Then Some,* visit their publishers website, www.hayhouse.com.

To learn more about loving yourself unconditionally, read *The Power is Within You* and *You Can Heal Your Life* by Louise Hay, www.louisehay.com.

For the book *Feel the Fear and Do it Anyway,* visit www.amazon.com or www.susanjeffers.com.

For the book *What You Think of Me is None of My Business,* visit www.amazon.com or www.terrycolewhittaker.com.

For the Emotional Guidance Scale by Abraham and Esther Hicks, visit www.abraham-hicks.com.

Contact Victoria Johnson at www.victoriajohnson.org/contact-victoria-johnson/.

ABOUT VICTORIA JOHNSON

Victoria is an internationally certified success coach with clients from all around the world. She is a graduate of multiple coaching programs, both in personal development and business coaching. Victoria is the National Teacher and Coach Trainer for Canada for Heal Your Life® Workshop Teachers and Coaches. Victoria supports and facilitates people through their spiritual and professional evolution based on the philosophies of Louise Hay.

Victoria loves to write—but her greatest passion is live training events. She is a certified business trainer in 'Managing with Heart and Mind' and 'Personality Dimensions' and has taught and trained in Canada, the USA, India, and the UK. She is available for corporate, non-profit, and keynote speaking and training events. As a graduate of the Dale Carnegie Leadership, Public Speaking and Coaching Program and a former corporate executive, Victoria teaches in a conversational style that uplifts and inspires people while providing plenty of "aha" moments.

Victoria is an entrepreneur who owns multiple franchises specializing in helping people overcome their addictions through laser therapy and support. She enjoys building businesses that empower and help others. Victoria is an addictions counselor who has helped thousands of people restore their health and relationships, and she is an active volunteer supporting those who advocate for victims of crime, tragedy and trauma.

She is the mother of two grown children and their partners. She and her partner, Chris, are grandparents to half a dozen beautiful children who keep them both inspired and focused on enjoying the present moment.

33657918R00139

Made in the USA
Middletown, DE
18 January 2019